ZYZZYVA

Volume XXXV, Number 3

Winter 2019

A SAN FRANCISCO JOURNAL OF ARTS AND LETTERS

SINCE 1985

ZYZZYVA

EDITOR
Laura Cogan

MANAGING EDITOR
Oscar Villalon

EDITORIAL ASSISTANT
Zack Ravas

SALES & MARKETING
Laura Howard

CONTRIBUTING EDITORS
Andrew Altschul, Sam Barry,
Robin Ekiss, John Freeman, Paul Madonna,
Ismail Muhammad, David L. Ulin

COPY EDITOR
Heather Hutson

INTERNS
Scout Turkel, Sophia Stewart, Gabriel Weiss

BOARD OF DIRECTORS
Warren Lazarow, *President*
Laura Cogan
Patrick Corman
Jane Gillette
Regis McKenna
Barbara Meacham
Jonathan Schmidt

ORIGINAL DESIGN
Three Steps Ahead

TYPE DESIGN
Text font created specially for
ZYZZYVA by Matthew Butterick

PRODUCTION
Josh Korwin

PRINTER
Versa Press, Inc.

DISTRIBUTION
Publishers Group West

SUBSCRIPTION SERVICES
EBSCO

ARCHIVES
Bancroft Library, UC Berkeley

CONTACT
57 Post St., #604, San Francisco, CA 94104
E contact@zyzzyva.org
W www.zyzzyva.org

SUBSCRIPTION
$42/four issues; $70/eight issues
Student rate: $30/four issues

ZYZZYVA (ISBN 978-1-73298-084-6) is published in April, August, and December by
ZYZZYVA, Inc., a nonprofit, tax-exempt corporation. © 2019 ZYZZYVA, Inc.

OUR PAPER STOCK is selected on the basis of its reduced
environmental impact. Text printed on Glatfelter Natures
Antique (30% post-consumer waste). Cover printed on
Kallima Coated Cover C2S. Both papers are FSC certified.

SPECIAL THANKS

Publication of this issue is made possible in part by the generous support of the National Endowment for the Arts and Amazon Literary Partnership.

CONTENTS

Letter from the Editor 19

FICTION

Charlie Jane Anders: This Is Why We Can't Have Nasty Things 105

Rita Bullwinkel: Andi Taylor vs. Artemis Victor 72

Lydia Conklin: Island of Beginnings 164

Ingrid Rojas Contreras: The Hand 162

        The Unfinished Question 163

Chia-Chia Lin: Ring Around the Equator, Pockets Full of Acres. 24

Andrew Roe: Is Someone Going to Say Something

        to the Woman Crying on BART?. 200

Nina Schuyler: Strangers. 120

FIRST TIME IN PRINT

Michael Sears: Channel 4 (fiction) 82

IN CONVERSATION

Desire, Text, and a San Francisco Apartment:

        Interview with Dodie Bellamy and Kevin Killian by Daniel Benjamin. 142

NONFICTION

Gloria Frym: Posthumous. 113

Nathan Heller: People in Process 94

Lydia Kiesling: Neighbors Talking 205

Paul Wilner: Unsentimental Education. 61

Mauro Aprile Zanetti: Lawrence Ferlinghetti: The Latin America Notebooks 181

POETRY

Meg Hurtado Bloom: We Californians 22

No Mesa Lasts Forever 23

W.S. Di Piero: Opening the Mail 69

The Smelters 70

Luiza Flynn-Goodlett: Object Permanence 93

Lady Nestor Gomez: In Love with a Woman 198

Making a Dentist Appointment 199

Sara Mumolo: Trauma Note 111

sam sax: Hangover 1.1.2019 58

Ode to the Young Queer Holding a Plant On the Train 59

Kevin Simmonds: Selfies 136

Upon Seeing an Old Photo of Sylvester 138

Matthew Zapruder: To the Bay Bridge 202

VISUAL ART

Janet Delaney, 97–104 • Lawrence Ferlinghetti, 185–197

FRONT & BACK COVERS

Cover artwork designed by Josh Korwin.

FORTHCOMING

No. 118 publishes in April, 2020.

Zyzzyva.

(ZIZ-zi-va) n. A San Francisco
literary journal; any of various
tropical American weevils of the
genus *Zyzzyva*. The last word in
the Oxford English Dictionary.

On View and Upcoming

Michael Jang's California

September 27, 2019 – January 18, 2020

A survey of Bay Area photographer Michael Jang, curated by Sandra S. Phillips

Orlando

February 7 – May 2, 2020

Guest curated by Tilda Swinton in partnership with Aperture

Open for exploration, contemplation, and engagement in the art and ideas of the McEvoy Family Collection

mcevoyarts.org
@mcevoyarts

1150 25th Street, Building B
San Francisco, CA 94107

THREE GROUNDBREAKING EXHIBITIONS
OF BAY AREA ARTISTS

Ron Nagle
Handsome Drifter

January 15–June 14, 2020

Rosie Lee Tompkins
A Retrospective

February 19–July 19, 2020

MATRIX 275
Sylvia Fein

Through March 1, 2020

BAMPFA

UC BERKELEY ART MUSEUM · PACIFIC FILM ARCHIVE
2155 Center St. | bampfa.org | @bampfa

COMMUNITY OF WRITERS

CELEBRATING FIFTY YEARS
IN THE HIGH SIERRA

SUMMER WRITING WORKSHOPS

Squaw Valley, California, near Lake Tahoe

POETRY WORKSHOP: JUNE 20-27, 2020

Camille Dungy ⊙ Robert Hass ⊙ Major Jackson
Ada Limón ⊙ Sharon Olds ⊙ Matthew Zapruder

WRITERS WORKSHOPS: JULY 6-13, 2020

Lisa Alvarez ⊙ Tom Barbash ⊙ Michael Jaime-Becerra ⊙ Max Byrd
Michael Carlisle ⊙ Mark Childress ⊙ Meg Waite Clayton ⊙ John Daniel
Leslie Daniels ⊙ Selden Edwards ⊙ Alex Espinoza ⊙ Richard Ford ⊙ Karen Joy Fowler
Joshua Ferris ⊙ Janet Fitch ⊙ Lynn Freed ⊙ Molly Giles ⊙ Sands Hall ⊙ Dana Johnson
Diane Johnson ⊙ Louis B. Jones ⊙ Anne Lamott ⊙ Dylan Landis
Michelle Latiolais ⊙ Krys Lee ⊙ Edie Meidav ⊙ Patricia K. Meyer
Kem Nunn ⊙ Kirstin Valdez Quade ⊙ Jason Roberts ⊙ Elizabeth Rosner
Margaret Wilkerson Sexton ⊙ Julia Flynn Siler ⊙ Martin J. Smith ⊙ Gregory Spatz
Elizabeth Tallent ⊙ Andrew Tonkovich ⊙ Amy Tan

Plus Literary Agents, Book & Literary Magazine Editors representing
Knopf ⊙ Little, Brown & Company
Riverhead Books ⊙ Santa Monica Review ⊙ ZYZZYVA and more

Financial Aid Available. Submissions Deadline: March 28, 2020.
www.communityofwriters.org | (530) 470-8440

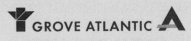

NoMad

HOTELS

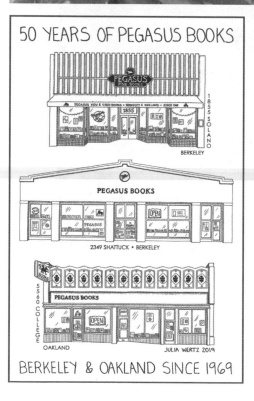

COMMUNITY SUPPORT
FOR LITERATURE & THE ARTS

Alexander Book Company

Bird & Beckett Books & Records

The Booksmith

City Arts & Lectures

City Lights Bookstore

Community of Writers of
   Squaw Valley

DIESEL, A Bookstore

Dolby Chadwick Gallery

Green Apple Books

Grove Atlantic

Harper Perennial

Heyday Books

Humboldt Distillery

McEvoy Foundation for the Arts

Mechanics' Institute

NoMad Hotels

Pegasus Books

San Francisco State University

Skylight Books

Stanford MFA

UC Berkeley Art Museum
   & Pacific Film Archive

University of San Francisco MFA

Virgin Hotels

ADDITIONAL SUPPORT PROVIDED BY

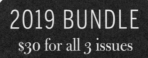

LETTER FROM THE EDITOR

Dear Reader,

One day in July I ran into a colleague on my way to lunch. We commiserated about the state of the world, briefly, and then he asked me if I'd been to the Flower Piano program at the San Francisco Botanical Garden yet. He said he'd just been, and that after one of the professional performers finished her set, a few of the people milling around took turns playing. One played David Bowie's "Life on Mars," singing softly under his breath. Another, a child of about ten, played a classical sonata, with astonishing beauty.

There's still art here, he said with a half smile as we parted ways. We're still here, I said in agreement.

It was only the second or third time someone had made a remark in that vein to me in the past few weeks.

There's a palpable sense that the pressure on creative folks in the San Francisco Bay Area is nearly intolerable—a widespread and reasonable feeling that is nevertheless at odds with the exceptional density of people still doing creative work of the highest caliber here. There's a sense that we're all hanging on by our fingertips, and maybe only the fingertips of one hand, while the other hand continues writing, continues playing.

Will the region that has always been our home endure as a generative hub of literary and artistic innovation? I want to say, Of course it will. But nothing is a given. If we don't make deliberate efforts to make the Bay Area a sustainable place for bakers and musicians, teachers and translators, poets and playwrights to live, we could see a major transformation, one that will incalculably diminish the fundamental identity of this place.

In the meantime, the pressure from the sense of transience and

20 the precariousness of it all naturally filters in and shapes the work we're seeing. As always, remarkable work can emerge from struggle and heartbreak, even from despair. We can celebrate that, but it's impossible not to worry about the cost. Because on the other side of that coin, the less romantic side, is all the unseen, unknowable work that could have been, but was stifled by lack of opportunity and support.

At a concert at the Fox Theater in Oakland in August, I chatted with a neighbor. The conversation quickly turned to lament, as it so often does: he's a San Francisco native, and grew up taking the N Judah out to Candlestick (more lamenting) to see the Giants play. He was living with family while searching for housing, he told me, and increasingly widening the search area. He paused and then said, "I'm not sure whether the Bay Area is really a place people live anymore. Maybe it's more of a temporary place to be for a few years." He was thinking of leaving the state entirely, maybe moving to Scottsdale, Arizona, so he could visit the Giants at spring training.

At times it seems there's as much despair about the inevitability of this transformation as there is about climate change: the decline is so far advanced and powerful in its own momentum, and the problem so expansive and multiform, and the leadership necessary to tackle it effectively and efficiently so lacking.

But then I'll find myself in a certain neighborhood, or in certain company, and somehow all that disruption seems muted or far off, as though the fog had cast a protective spell on that corner of the Bay.

And if it's not a foregone conclusion, if such pockets of neighborhoods and community persevere, then we have to try to protect the culture that we still have.

With that in mind, and on the cusp of our 35th anniversary next year, we bring you an issue dedicated to this unique place. If for you, too, it sometimes feels that this transformation of home is already a *fait accompli*, I hope this sampling, drawn from the wealth of our local talent, from all stages of career and across genres, pushes back against that notion—and, in so doing, makes an eloquent case for all we stand to lose, and all we must invest in conserving.

Some of us are still here; others have left. Some are poised to go, reluctantly or bitterly or enthusiastically seeking new terrain. Amid the tension and pressure, amid the injustice and anxiety, art and literature endure and blossom in the Bay Area with uncommon ingenuity, vision, and persistence.

Yours,

L.

WE CALIFORNIANS

MEG HURTADO BLOOM

We never admit we have a problem.
We compress. We knead. We withdraw toxins.
Sun-blind and blond-hearted,
we hang around Valhalla,
keeping old warriors alive.

It's all super-casual. Our host,
the spectral Spanish king—
whose every vein burned blue as winter wind,
who left us names for every hillside—
has betrothed us to the Coast. Her beauty
keeps our tempers cool as gold
forgotten in a sea cave.

We trade treasure for mirage, mirage for treasure.
We kill our captors, mindfully, and move on,
knowing we have nothing:
just one wave and then another,
then another. Maybe rain.

Admittedly, we pay too much attention to the stars,
knowing ourselves future smithereens,
space dust in progress.
Love ends up on the cutting room floor,
but so does evil. So does madness. So does night.

NO MESA LASTS FOREVER

MEG HURTADO BLOOM

When I was young it was rare to see the desert on TV,
my own mad planet, open on all sides,

dirt red as sores split by neon creosote.
The desert is a million ways to die, but framing is everything.

Wile E. Coyote teaches, Never look down as you cross canyons.
The cloud that sustains you may not extend beyond your ankles,

but so what? Imaginary landscapes manifest for
the pure of heart. Fulfill the fantasy that you are so tough

you can dine on tin cans, smartly carved. Then sweep it away,
start hunting. Desire is all there is. Desire is enough.

When you finally catch up, you'll just stand there.
That train you imagined has come.

Meg Hurtado Bloom is the editor at Hologram Press and lives in San Francisco.

RING AROUND THE EQUATOR, POCKETS FULL OF ACRES

CHIA-CHIA LIN

When Delepine first started running, the air shredded her lungs. Like inhaling powdered glass. After a run, she kept right on sweating and her face kept coloring, peaking at its maximum carmine hue when she was doing something embarrassingly low-impact, like sitting at her desk and rattling the pencils in her cup. She was an assistant at a design firm, and the last thing that belonged with all the high-gloss furniture and filmy blouses was her inflamed, oddly porous face.

It was ludicrous she was running at all—and more so that at thirty, she was running alongside Eva. Eva, for whom running seemed as easy and restful as sleep. Eva, who could turn her dark eyes to the scenery— eucalyptus tree, sea cliff, rolling hill. Her body lean, movements fluid, footsteps light.

They had met in the mid-nineties in a continuing education class, Intro to the Internet for Business. Delepine's firm had sent her when her boss had fallen sick, but Eva, an ER nurse, was there on her own. Eva scorned the men who spoke up in class. On the first day, a pigeon had flown into the classroom, and she had swatted it with her notebook and then chased it out by flapping her windbreaker behind it like a giant pigeon herself.

On the third class, during the fifteen-minute break, Delepine and Eva walked to a pond and back. It was a paltry thing, the size of a parking space, but they stood at the edge and peered at the algae, which clumped in places like pureed peas. It had been a week of bombings—yesterday, a letter bomb in Sacramento, said to be the Unabomber's work; last Wednesday, Oklahoma City, with the death count still rising. Delepine never knew what to say about tragedies; she'd end up sounding mawkish or flippant. She could only think in images: the nine-story hole, papers from file cabinets blowing down the rubbled street, a toy truck covered in ash. Eva told her a man had plunged seven floors in an elevator during the blast and emerged unscathed. Another man crawled under his desk while, beside him, the floor dropped away.

Week after week, they walked to the pond on their breaks. Eva was thinking of starting a home care business. Just an idea. Just a thought.

They both lived in the East Bay at the time, and they started to walk, then jog, outside of class. Suddenly, Delepine realized, Eva was racing. She was not racing Delepine—there was no point to that. But she clenched her teeth and fixed her eyes on a point far down the road. When she reached it, she chose another spot, a rock or shadow, and ran for that, too, in a way that made Delepine wonder what was at stake.

All she knew was that Eva had grown up in Texas, in a tiny, mostly Latino town an hour's drive from Odessa. During summer floods, cantaloupes from the farms floated down the streets. Later they rotted in the sun. Her father disappeared with her brother, leaving behind a house full of women. Eva was different from her five sisters. She was slender, not religious, not a mother, far from home. In the summer, when Delepine tanned, she felt they could have been sisters, too, even if Eva's dark spirals of hair stood in sharp contrast to Delepine's thin wheat-colored strands.

26   Sometimes Eva said, "I came out of nothing." She looked Delepine straight on, eyes squinted to sharpen the gaze.

A few months into their runs, Delepine found a free book in a bin, a paperback from ten years ago, *Running for Women,* written mostly by a man.

> *The broad pelvic girdle of women inclines them toward straddle-legged running. Women, therefore, should try to run with their legs as close together as possible, especially on flat turf or pavement.*

If you are attacked by a rapist on a run:
The first thing you should do is to begin a controlled scream.

If you are confronted by an exhibitionist:
Don't give him the satisfaction of a shocked look.

There was also a bewildering section titled Hair Removal for the Underarms. Delepine used the book as a training manual anyway, though she never mentioned it to Eva. Week 1: five-minute warm-up, six 300-yard jogs alternated with 100-yard walks, five-minute warm-down. By week 12, she could toss off a half-hour run—not a jog, not a trot, but a sustained, honest run.

They tried a few 5Ks, and as the months and then two years ticked by, moved on to 10K street races, 10K trails up and down the headlands of the North Bay, half marathons, marathons. Eva was fast. Once she took fifth in their age group. Other times, eighth and ninth. The real surprise was, Delepine was no longer slow. She thought of her old Phys Ed teacher, a squat man who stretched his sweat-wicking clothing to capacity. During the rope-climbing unit, he looked up their shorts, or so some said, and he was chummy with the girls. But Delepine he only mocked, saying as she was lapped by the whole class, "There goes our track star," and, "Guess someone's on the rag."

In the constant running they now did was a certain hunkering down, a blindered resolve or grit. Once Delepine had pounded out the first ten or twenty steps, all thoughts vacated her mind, except how many miles had been covered, how many were left. On the uphill, how much was left until the downhill. Math and estimation: the percentage finished, the approximate time left, the pace so far, and on and on. She never questioned whether they would finish, only how long it would take and how much it would hurt.

It mimicked her life at work, when she calculated the hours until lunch, or how much of the day was left, or how much of the week or year. But her new athletic life was a different kind of life. A second, better life? Some kind of answer to her first. It had the quality of immense potential. Their times were getting shorter, their distances longer, their bodies more compact. Their lungs were expanding. Everything was expanding.

Delepine moved to the South Bay but continued to meet Eva on the weekends. Sometimes they met halfway, on the San Francisco side, and ran the Golden Gate Bridge; Delepine counted its steel suspender ropes every fifty feet as they appeared out of the fog. Other times, they jogged through the dry hills of Fremont or Milpitas, keeping to paved paths after a brush with poison oak.

Delepine's husband, Rodney, was an estate lawyer who had grown up in the woods of Washington, in a town of several hundred. He liked routines—blistering coffee and sci-fi books before bed, public radio in the morning. He had a heft to him, mostly in the chest and shoulders; he was a bit hunched, a bit lumbering, but not unfit. Although he refused to run, he enjoyed bikes and activities that involved hurling things. Pitching. Bowling. In high school he'd been passable at shot put. They'd met at a singles event; ghost-blue jellyfish pulsed in a tank over a shelf of liquor. From one end of the bar, Rodney smiled at her

28   apologetically and dug his drink into his soft stomach.

A few months later, Eva met Sean on an ER night shift, the shift heaviest on the psychos, she'd said. Sean had made a turn too fast on his motorcycle and slid across an asphalt road. Eva walked into the exam room, snatched his arm, spread lidocaine jelly on the road rash, and scrubbed it of debris. Sean asked, "Would it kill you to be more gentle?" She brushed the inside of his wrist with one knuckle. After her shift he took her to Denny's, where they both polished off Grand Slams.

They tried double dates. But when they went to a steak tavern to celebrate the new year, Sean spent half the night at the bar, smoking with a vet who sputtered, "It's my American God-given right to pollute my own damn lungs!" Sean shouted, "If not at a bar, then where?" They were louder than the music. The bartender retrieved a hidden ashtray and set it between the two men.

After he slid back into the booth, Sean spent the rest of the night relaying his close calls, such as the time he'd tried to pass between two big rigs that had nearly sandwiched him. "But the best save," he said, "was when I skidded across two lanes in the rain. My bike was sideways. Sideways!" He smacked the table open-palmed. "My knee kissed the ground. We're talking pucker factor 9.9."

Eva shook her head into her glass of seven and seven, but one side of her mouth slid up. She was wearing a red tank top that cut in at her slim waist, tight jeans, sneakers. Not fashionable, really, but men were felled by that combination of sexiness and approachability. Delepine was wearing her work clothes, a blazer over a top with an asymmetrical neckline. In the bathroom a girl had asked where she'd gotten her chandelier earrings.

In the corner of the tavern, under a light that changed from purple to blue to green, a bald Filipino man sat at a piano and tilted his head toward a mic. Between songs, he pulled his suit sleeves up and dabbed at the gleaming spot of colored light on his forehead. He started "Make You Feel My Love." Eva snickered. Delepine smiled, too, but when he sang, "I'd go hungry, I'd go black and blue," she trembled. Maybe it was the warmth of the four or five glasses of wine. Or the stripe of light across the tines of her fork. The man sang it extraordinarily low, and he'd smoothed over the ruts of Bob Dylan's voice. It was stupid. Live music in a steakhouse under a disco light. But she could not stop watching this man leaning into the piano, consumed by his song, unaware of their table, his phrases trailing into whispers. Delepine began to sweat. What were they doing there? How many hours had they been sitting around talking about nothing? Time was precious, and they were meant for more.

"Oh no," she said when Sean tried to top off her wine. "I need to run tomorrow morning."

"Tomorrow's Sunday," he said and steadied her glass with one hand.

Delepine covered her glass.

Eva took the bottle. "Leave a girl alone." She poured the wine into her own glass, finishing it off. The shadows on her bare arm made her deltoids prominent, and Delepine wondered if she'd added weights to her regimen.

When Sean grabbed the check, Delepine eyed her husband. She had told him that Sean was between jobs again.

Rodney pulled the billfold over. "You get it next time."

"Let me at it."

"Next time."

Sean lunged across the table and snatched the bill out of Rodney's hands. Delepine's water glass sloshed but did not spill.

Sean laughed. "Work on those reflexes, buddy."

When they began training for their first triathlon, Delepine started a log. She tracked the distances she had swum, biked, run. On a whim,

30 she added a row to the spreadsheet that calculated how far she'd gone around the equator. In the first month, she logged 320 miles—1.3 percent of the way.

That winter, Delepine and Eva attempted their first open water swim in the part of the bay called Aquatic Park—a name that conjured grass and sun and baby marine mammals, rather than its actual murk and aching cold. Before they entered the water, they struggled into wetsuits in the women's locker room of the Dolphin Club. Delepine's fingers were stiff from working the neoprene rubber up her calves, creating a pinch of slack and trying to slide it up her thighs without losing it; repeat and repeat. Slow as a python's hinged jaw. Still the crotch of the suit was too low, restricting the movement of her legs. Her heart was already pounding, and all she had done so far was catch a glimpse of the ocean, a whiff of the dank sand.

"Piece of shit's two sizes too small." Eva was hopping on one foot beside her, clawing at the ankle of her own rental suit, though they'd been warned against using their fingernails.

Across the bench was a woman, sixty-odd years and naked, a specimen of pure feminine strength, all smoothed-down musculature. Brown sinewy arms and neck. Flat, pale breasts like two gel packs. A seasoned Athena about to dive into a sea of open-mouthed beasts. "You've got to get it higher up your legs before you start yanking on it like that," she said. "Plastic bags on the feet. Helps you slide them through." She pulled on a hunter green racerback, then snapped her cap over her shaved gray head. None of the adjustments and stuffing of hair.

"That all you wearing?" Delepine asked. Staring at those bare legs, the loose, speckled skin over sculpture.

"You get used to it," the Athena said.

Fifteen minutes later, they approached the shore. The wind cut at Delepine's face and hands. Could she do this—shed her towel and enter the brown water? Within shouting distance was a couple sitting on a blanket, wrapped in two more blankets: the woman leaned deep into the man. Only the red pom-pom of her hat was left out in the cold.

She toed the water. "Oh."

Eva walked a few inches in. She whispered a few angry curses, then laughed. She broke into a run, squealed, and when the water was deep enough, went under.

The prospect of being left behind made Delepine move. She kicked up sprays, stumbled, fell on her hands and knees. She plunged all the way in, though it was still shallow and her thighs dragged on sand. Thrashed further in. Hands and feet burning. A headache spread to her face, stretched her skin there much too tight. Water entered her suit from the back of her neck, shooting down a line of ice. Her lungs shrank and refused to hold air. She could see only a few inches of her arms, which disappeared after the elbows, and truly, nothing else was visible. It was not like the darkness of night, in which forms slowly manifested themselves. In the water, the world constricted once and did not release.

She tried to collect herself. She stopped, treaded water, searched for her friend among the waves. Ten yards away, Eva's little head turned for breaths too quickly. Her goggles became bug-eyed fear. Her open mouth took up half her face. In that inflated mouth, an expression Delepine had never seen before, on anyone: survival, ambition, nakedness, greed. The hungry sucking down of oxygen.

Who could remember to point the toes, turn the elbows up, angle the curve of the hand so the pinky entered first, assess which direction the waves were coming from so you could breathe out the other side?

The waves pushed them back as they propelled themselves forward; were they advancing at all? In the pool where they'd practiced, water was something you could move—you pressed it away with your hands.

Here, it was something else. All the flailing in the world and still it would not yield. After only a third of a mile, they scrabbled to shore. Just behind them: a sidewalk, a grassy hill, the huge Ghirardelli sign on scaffolding, beckoning to tourists with the promise of sludgy hot chocolate. They gasped on their little stretch of sand, encased in their wetsuits, dripping water in the winter wind, crazed, wild, unreasonable.

They watched the silver-capped head of their Athena. She bobbed at a steady rhythm, far out in the bay, farther than they dared to go. Her bare arms flashed and sliced the water. She might as well have been flying.

Trying to lose the twenty pounds he'd put on, Rodney began riding his old hybrid bike each morning along Stevens Creek, a tiny stream that led toward the bay. Delepine joined him. At six-thirty in the morning, the path was mostly empty and they could pedal at liberating speeds on the long, straight stretches.

The terrain out there was experimental, alien. Along the path were a giant NASA wind tunnel complex and engine test stand, Moffett Airfield, abandoned hangars. Everything exposed. Pylons rose from the grasses, and power lines drooped between them and zigzagged across the marsh.

Delepine's favorite spot was a bench along the path, right at the edge of the bay. Dumbarton Bridge all the way across the water, barely arched. The salt ponds opened up, and mallards and white pelicans waded in the brackish water, resting mid-migration. From a distance, the birds were snowy and clean.

"Nice ride," Rodney said. He removed his helmet. His hair was matted down and his squarish head clearly outlined by the bright blue sky. At times like this, she wanted to laugh at the simplicity of a good life; they worked, and felt good for working. They'd talked about kids: maybe, not just now. They contributed tiny, matched amounts each month to 401Ks, which they invested into their neighbors, the dot-com companies. It was almost like they were part of it, the technology boom, the excitement of ideas. Delepine leaned her bike against the bench and ran up to him. He draped an arm around her and ducked so he could kiss her. Their helmets knocked.

33

Half a year after she'd started the log, she was 9.5 percent of the way around the equator.

Delepine and Eva took Rodney on one of their long training rides in the East Bay. They biked along two-lane roads in single file. Whoever was in front pointed out the cracks in the asphalt, stray branches, litter. The other two drafted off the first. They took turns pulling at the front. It was orderly. Together, they pursued the end of the ride.

Forty miles in, a long ascent began. Gaps spread between them; they would meet at the top. "Take it slow," Delepine called back to Rodney, who was spinning on his lowest gear, expressionless below his helmet. Eva was already far ahead, crusading, trying to destroy the mountain. Her low, curly ponytail shivered with her efforts.

The climb was longer than Delepine remembered. The road was winding and even the occasional car climbed slowly. The hill steepened, and she stood up on the pedals. A minute later that became difficult, too, so she sat back down and shifted to her lowest gear. She hated being on the last gear; there was no recourse left. You'd finish the hill on that gear, or you wouldn't.

The summer day was sweltering. Trees were few. They were unprotected from the sun. A mixture of sweat and sunscreen was drying in layered streaks on her arms. When she blinked, her eyes stung.

She glanced back at Rodney. His whole body was wobbling with each stomp of the pedals. He was leaning too heavily on his arms. His front wheel fishtailed.

She kept going. She and Eva never rested on a steep climb. It was not pride, so much. More that it could be impossible to start up again.

34 She had once rested partway up Mount Tam, on a very high grade. Then she pedaled a half rotation and toppled over. Got back on her bike, pedaled twice, and fell over again. After that, when it got bad, she biked through tears.

In her peripheral vision, a row of dry, scrappy bushes along the road bent and wavered in the heat.

After several miles of straight climbing, Delepine turned to check on Rodney again and saw him far down the hill, crumpled over his bike on the shoulder of the road. She wrenched her bike around, rode down, unclipped, and rushed to him. He was wheezing, almost hissing on the ends of inhales. She extricated his bike so he could lie in the open.

There were no cars around. "Take it easy," Delepine said. "Catch your breath." She tried to sound calm, but when she retrieved her cell phone from her saddle bag, she saw the slashed phone icon—no service in the mountains. She stared at the small greenish-gray screen. She looked up the hill for Eva, who'd disappeared.

When his breathing was less labored, Delepine helped him sit up. She rubbed his damp back. The top of his head had a sour smell.

"How do you feel?" she asked.

"Cramps." Rodney hugged his knees. His eyes were closed.

Delepine pulled one of the mounted water bottles from his bike and handed it to him. "You almost made it. We're a half-mile from the top," she said, though it was more like two miles.

Rodney opened his eyes. "I can't make it half a mile."

"That's okay. Drink."

Rodney took a small sip. The water gurgled as he flipped the bottom up.

She heard the whisper of brakes and looked up to see Eva skidding to a stop. "What happened?"

"Seems like we overdid it in the heat," Delepine said.

Eva rested her bike on its side. She knelt down, felt Rodney's forehead, then pressed her fingers to his inner wrist. "Did you throw up?"

"No."

"Dizzy?"

"A little."

Eva pointed at the bottle in his hand, and then at the full one still mounted to his bike. "Those should be almost empty by now."

Rodney shrugged. "You guys didn't stop for a water break."

"Drink while you're riding." Eva stood up. She retrieved her own water bottle, a third full. "You're dehydrated. Maybe a little heat stroke. I don't think it's serious, but let's cool you off. Del, help him with his shirt."

Delepine leaned close to him. Rodney blinked rapidly. She eased his shirt off. His broad chest was splotched pink. His stomach puckered where he was holding it in.

Eva squirted the rest of her water on him. It dried in a minute.

A blue hatchback stopped beside them. A woman with blond hair like a mushroom cap and shiny red lips rolled down her window. "You girls okay?"

"We're fine," Eva said. "But can you give him a ride? Do you have anything salty to eat?"

Rodney scrambled up and pulled his shirt back on.

The woman agreed to drive him back to where they'd parked. They wedged his bike into the rear, but there wasn't room for another bike. Delepine turned to Rodney. "I'd go with you if I could."

He nodded and climbed into the passenger seat. Delepine waved. As the hatchback pulled away, she saw him lift and shake his hands. He was being funny. His specialty was self-deprecation. The woman was laughing, dipping her nose almost to the steering wheel.

Eva shook her head. "For the love of God, Del, get him a road bike.

36 That clunker he's grinding on weighs more than my car."

"He loves that bike." It was no use explaining that a new bike would mean seven, eight hundred dollars. Delepine had tried to tell her before that there were only five people in Rodney's firm, that it wasn't the kind of law firm Eva was thinking of. Plus they were saving for a house now.

Delepine and Eva had bought their wetsuits and road bikes used, but still it had been a chunk of cash. Then: helmet, goggles, cap, replacement sneakers after the treads wore down, bike shoes, bike gloves, pedals, sunglasses that hooked around the ears. Tights that padded against chafing. The one-piece suit you wore under everything, so you could peel off your wetsuit as you ran out of the ocean, then jump on your bike still dripping. To use the bathroom, though, you had to strip naked.

On the road, when they saw Italian bikes—ridden by older men carrying mass in their midsections, wearing tights that made them look even more top-heavy as they balanced on the 23-millimeter tires—Eva made a scoffing noise, almost a growl, and set off on a sprint. Straining against their inferior bikes, they passed the men in seconds. Eva wouldn't have said a word about Rodney's bike if he had just kept up.

Eva righted her bike and waited until Delepine was ready. They started the ascent again. Delepine pushed herself harder; Rodney would be waiting. Her breaths quickened and deepened. Her quads burned as she drove herself to the cusp of something. The hill ended.

As they started the downhill, they moved their hands from the brake hoods to the drops. They crouched low and tucked their elbows in. The road unfurled for them. Side by side, they flew, taking the switchbacks fast, raising the foot on the inside of a turn, skimming the center line without crossing it. On this side of the mountain, they were faster than the cars. So fast the smallest movement of handlebars could end in disaster. Steady, steady.

That night, Rodney made his coffee, then climbed into bed beside her. He read a few chapters of his book, about a crippled king with a healthy clone-twin, and then placed it facedown on the bed. "Why didn't you guys take any water breaks?" he asked.

"We usually hydrate while we're riding."

"I don't know how to do that."

"Do it on a flat part, with no turns. Reach down to the cage while you're pedaling. Maybe move your other hand toward the stem for balance."

"Have you ever seen me do that?"

She chewed on her bottom lip to stop herself from saying something harsh. "I'm sorry. I didn't think of it."

"I was so thirsty."

He studied the cover of his book. On it were two identical faces staring at each other against a galactic backdrop. "I don't think I'll go on any more rides with you two."

She wanted to tell him that he had done something she had not. He'd pushed himself past his actual, physical abilities. She didn't know what that was like. She was not as brave; she always held back; she pushed until it hurt and then stopped—she never pushed to that threadbare state.

"You did well," she said quietly, but he only blew air out of his mouth.

She switched off the lamp and slipped one hand up his shirt, feeling his smooth, dry chest and the twitchings of his heart. She put her nose in his neck, which always seemed a little sticky. She paused, then slid her hand down to his stomach, then into his shorts. Rodney did not move, and for a moment she thought he'd turn away. But he reached for her.

Delepine was laid off and then hired at another firm. She worked alongside two other assistants, both a decade younger. She became a senior assistant. She had once hoped to be a designer.

One of them, Greta, with translucent skin and long, fluttering hair and a way of talking that seemed to use only the tip of her tongue,

38   asked Delepine about her plans for the weekend.

"I'm doing a triathlon."

"You're *what*," Greta said. She wrinkled the supple skin of her face beyond a normal level of dubiousness.

It was true Delepine did not look like a triathlete, or an athlete of any kind. She was more fit than she had ever been in her life; she could jog for hours and hours. But she had a different kind of body from Eva's. A large ribcage, for one. Her muscles tended to bulk instead of lengthen. And when she was hungry, she ate what she wanted—packages of cookies, chips covered in cheese dust. Salads and mandarin oranges didn't cut it for her after she had swum a mile and a half, the way they did for Eva. That stuff wasn't fuel; it was foliage.

"It's my first," Delepine said.

Greta leaned across Delepine's desk. Both of the new assistants liked to drape themselves on things. And they were always stretching at their desks. They carried yoga mats in single-strap bags. Their generation, evidently, was limber. Greta pursed her lips. "Cool."

At the triathlon, Delepine and Eva started themselves at the back of the last wave, with the most apprehensive of the beginners. It was a mistake. The swim across that bit of ocean was like navigating a shipwreck scene. Some people weren't even swimming the crawl; they were dog-paddling and breast-stroking and making unrecognizable motions with their flailing arms. Delepine lost sight of Eva early on and felt utterly alone in the crush of bodies. Her wetsuit compressed her chest. Black sheathed limbs churned around her. There was no space, no air. She forgot to keep sighting for the buoy, and swam an arc instead of a line. At the huge inflated buoy, she tried to cut the corner too close, and was pressed into it by ten or twelve others making the turn, so that she briefly thought she would suffocate with her face in the plastic.

A woman three yards ahead of her shouted for help. A rescue kayak slid into Delepine's path, and an oar just missed her head.

Disorientation: she couldn't find where she had racked her bike. She got on without her helmet and had to dismount. When she finished the ride and returned to the transition area, she forgot again where her rack was, and had to run her bike back and forth along the aisle, looking for her periwinkle towel. Then she put on her sneakers and swiped more sunscreen at her face, and took off running in the opposite direction of the course. Her biking legs buckled, surprised by the hard, ungiving ground.

Both the bike and run courses were loops; she didn't see Eva once. But at the finish line, there she was in her black-and-green tri suit, hollering at Delepine, waving a half-eaten banana in the air.

They traded stories. A man swimming beside Eva had tired out midway and clung to her as though she were the edge of a pool. "Get off me!" Eva shouted. She might have kicked him in the stomach. She flagged a kayak for him, then left him bobbing and continued on to swim her fastest time yet, just trying to get out of the water.

Delepine had not been fast. Well, she had finished, anyway.

Training days were one of two types: easy or hard. On easy days, they slowed themselves down until they had that feeling—they could go on like this for eons. Hard days meant pushing—their bodies could not bear one second more. They wanted more than their bodies could give.

Delepine knew she was holding Eva back; she just was not as fast. So at the turn of the century, she upped her intervals. Two-minute jog, one-minute dead run. Two-lap glide, one-lap turbine burst. Every time you came to an uphill on your bike, you wrung out your lungs and scorched rubber. She had trouble summoning the energy for these sprints until she realized where it lay—in deep, covered wells. *Anger. Desire.* Cravings for more. For Greta to be afraid of her, instead of leaning on her desk, running her long, smooth fingers all over Delepine's things.

40 For the thirteen-year-old boy who had called her "mama bitch" on the street to see the full, ugly beast of her fury. For their real estate agent to stop pushing them into a neighborhood of old slaughterhouses. For speed—pure, raging speed. So that she would no longer be slow.

Rodney left for two weeks and came back to her. All she knew was that the woman was younger. Delepine pictured her as Greta.

At night she sat beside Rodney on the couch and watched Ground Zero smolder on television, day after day. She'd close her eyes and try to sleep, then think of the jumpers instead. Rodney would fidget beside her, too alert. He was still tiptoeing around the house, cringing when he stacked a dish too loudly. She had not touched him for a month. He'd shed thirty pounds on a low-carb diet and he looked good—she could see how he was more attractive now than when she'd met him, more distinguished with the steely bristles in his hair, more effortless in the clothing she'd helped him pick—but he did not look like him. Sometimes she watched him from another room and from a certain angle he was Rodney again, which made her think, you, you were capable of that?

Delepine and Eva fell into a rhythm of three triathlons every summer. They developed techniques they believed in, like double capping when the water was below sixty, putting on their goggles between the two cap layers, breast-stroking the last fifty yards to warm up the legs for biking.

Each race had its own drama, with cramping, currents, heat, flat tires, or just a badly digested breakfast. Panic appeared unpredictably. One race in San Diego, everyone was talking about a shark sighting. During the bike portion of a race in Tahoe, the sky blackened and dumped down rain, and they shivered so hard on a long descent they could barely squeeze the brakes. Eva was hit in the face by a cutting board as she swam from Alcatraz Island.

Every good thing they experienced felt hard-earned. When they

biked up a mountain and reached the top, the downhill was what they
reaped—that fast, flying portion, when they hunched low over the handlebars and let the wind enfold them. Their hunger was cavernous and food was not just nourishment, but the deepest possible fulfillment. After they swam, they warmed themselves with a tepid shower that ran down their skin like hot tropical rain.

While everyone else, it seemed, was raising children, this was what they did. It was not a domestic world, nor a world of men, nor of careers or recognition. It was both a selfish and passionate world, without a thought of anyone else, for the two of them alone. They were still young, but old enough to know that in the real world, they had compromised on who they were. In this world, they were dazzling.

Sean was killed in a motorcycle accident on a narrow winding road in the East Bay hills. He'd made a wide turn, creeping into the incoming lane, and a car had clipped him.

Delepine slept in Eva's living room. She cooked terrible dinners in the unfamiliar kitchen. Runny quiches, leathery pork chops. Eva ate everything.

"Do you think I should submit an obituary?"

Delepine stared at her. "I don't know how these things work."

"This is what my grandmother's obituary said: 'She is survived by seven children, twenty-nine grandchildren, seventy-four great-grandchildren, and ninety-two great-great-grandchildren.'" Eva cackled.

Delepine studied a framed drawing of a wild horse that hung above the kitchen table. She knew Sean had drawn it, but she had trouble imagining him sitting still long enough to finish it. There was fine, meticulous pencil work, with crosshatching on the long underside of the mustang. It was rearing up, its head twisted back to look at the sky.

"You ever been to a rodeo?" Eva asked.

"No."

"They're stupid. But the tacos, oh God, the tacos de alambre, with the meat cut right off the skewers—you're eating these tacos and watching cowboys from out of town, these white boys with boots that make them walk like ducks. But once they're on that bull, you can't stop watching them. The bull's like this huge flexing muscle, and they're like a piece of lint hanging on. One of my sisters would follow the cowboys around all night, then end up with some Mexican kid from the high school rodeo team."

Eva got up, retrieved an uncapped bottle of bourbon, and sat back down. She offered Delepine the first swig. Delepine drank. Rodney was probably in bed reading. He might even be asleep, an arm hooked over his head, the skin around one eye crinkling against the pillow. He'd be turned toward her side of the bed.

"The obituary," Eva said. "What should I do about the obituary?" She ran her finger over a glossy knot in the oak table. "Just a few words. Can you help me? How and why he died."

The next morning, one week after Sean's death, Eva appeared downstairs, fully dressed in her running clothes. They headed to Tilden Park. The paved four-mile path led them through peeling eucalyptus trees, herds of cows, and sections of dense, settled fog. There were vista points, but on that morning little could be seen apart from the path. Parts of the run were like rushing blind.

Eva ran, and Delepine followed. When they reached the end, they turned around. When they reached the beginning, they turned around again. In the white abyss, Eva's figure was the only thing visible. Delepine tracked the lime green soles of Eva's sneakers.

Eva came to a stop after thirty-two miles. She stretched. Delepine bent over and massaged her kneecaps. They hobbled back to the car.

"That fog," Eva said.

"How do you feel?"

"Like there's something I can't outrun."

When she got home and logged the miles, Delepine realized she'd finished. She tried to rustle up a feeling of accomplishment, of momentousness. She'd gone once around the world, powered by nothing but herself. And now she was exactly where she'd started.

Weekday mornings, Delepine tucked in an hour's swim before work. At the office she grew sleepy around two or three in the afternoons. A leaden weight swept over her. Hunger buzzed in the pit of her stomach.

"Food coma," Greta said. "It's the carbs. I saw your mac and cheese today. You want to go for the slow-burning stuff."

Delepine ran a hand down her face. The smell of chlorine was permanently embedded in her skin. She watched Greta slide between two desks and head for the bathroom. Her movements were part of a slow and secret dance.

Delepine shifted papers at her desk and patted her hair. It was getting brittle. She didn't know if it was the chlorine or just age. Rodney marveled that he'd never once seen a gray hair on her head, but sometimes when she untangled a section with her fingers, she'd find broken strands in her hand. She'd tried slathering all sorts of things on her hair—mashed avocado, olive oil, egg yolk, honey.

At least her lung capacity was increasing. And her heart was getting stronger. She had read somewhere that when you exercised like this, your heart grew. It was a muscle, after all; it enlarged.

Two years later, Eva slept with a doctor at work and got pregnant.

"Oh?" Delepine said. Eva had just turned forty-one; Delepine was forty-two.

"It's not like I wanted it," Eva said.

"I didn't—"

"But now I do want it."

"The race in March—"

"Still on."

Eva wanted to name him Hyperion after the tallest known tree in the world, discovered that past summer on a remote slope of the Redwood National Forest. The tree was 371 feet tall, which defied scientific understanding of how water was pulled so far against gravity. The only way to verify its height had been to climb it while carrying a fiberglass measuring tape and a two-way radio.

During their weekend sessions, Eva was shorter of breath. "Like training at a higher elevation," she said. People stared at her, not always with approval.

For the last five months of Eva's pregnancy, Delepine was finally faster in all three events. In fact, she'd always been the better swimmer. Eva kicked a little too hard to be efficient, and when she breathed, she wrenched her head too far out of the water. But the bias of the triathlon favored cyclists and then runners after that. You were on a bike three times as long as you were in the water. Plus the panic erased Delepine's swimming skills on race day. And maybe, after all, she was not more skilled, just more buoyant.

It was an easy birth; baby Hippie slid out in two hours. On the day she was to leave the hospital, Eva handed the baby to Delepine, then snuck into the stairwell. For ten minutes, she ran stairs. When she heard footsteps, she slowed to a respectable walk.

Delepine finished her second loop around the equator. It did not seem possible at forty-two, or post-pregnancy, but they were both getting faster. Sometimes Eva brought Hippie along in a sleek black racing stroller, an aerodynamic three-wheel contraption that coasted like a sky-bound chariot. He flopped against the back with his mouth open to the wind and his soft hair blown to the side. Delepine thought how lucky he was, pushed by the fastest mother in the world. What made them keep on like this? That one life was not enough. Maybe this was the rarest sort of love, uncomplicated and unshakable. Eva was her steady partner, the love of her second life, a companion through every conceivable thing.

By eighteen months, Hippie was madly in love with Delepine. When she left the room for something, he called, "Didi, didi, didi." Nonstop, like an alarm. No one had taught him that. But he was a little slow, Eva said. He'd just started walking, and he didn't like it so much. He didn't seem to know how to smile. When Delepine arrived on the weekends, he did a sort of twist and baby side bend and said, "Didi!" with his head near the carpet. The euphoria so fierce it was almost panic. He lifted one foot and tumbled down. She picked him up. She liked to squeeze his legs, which looked like they'd been sectioned off with string. He mashed his face into her chin. When she put him down and reached for the door to leave, his face crumpled. No one had taught him these things.

Rodney sometimes watched him while they went out for a ride. Before Hippie came over, Rodney always moved the coffee table into their bedroom. He vacuumed the kitchen. When she and Eva returned, Rodney spoke in a way she was unused to. Delepine wondered how they spent those mornings.

"Don't even mention it," he said. "What a sweet boy. What a darling." He pulled Delepine to his side and squeezed her shoulders hard.

When they all went out for lunch, Hippie squirmed against Eva and shot his arms out for Delepine. Eva rolled her eyes and handed him over. As they waited for a table or walked to the parking lot, strangers smiled at Delepine. Knowing smiles. Once, as they walked through a shopping center, a mother stopped, placed her baby girl's face right in front of Hippie's, and said, "Hi, baby," in a helium voice. The babies made creaky whines, the kind that prefaced crying. The mother cocked her head at Delepine and asked, "How old's yours?"

46 "One and a half," Eva said from five feet away.

Delepine smiled. She walked slower and slower and fell behind. She and Rodney had avoided the subject of children in the years after his affair. She put her face close to Hippie's. He looked like he was hiding a meatball in each cheek. He wrapped his puffy arms around her neck. He was the only one who saw her try not to cry.

They saved and trained for a year, then flew to a Half Ironman in Puerto Rico. They had never left the continental U.S. before; after dropping Hippie off, they grasped each other by the elbows and squealed like girls. Two hours into the flight, they soared over a molten river at sunset. The land was dull and dusted brown, but the gold switchbacking rope of water glinted.

It was a long, gorgeous race. They swam Condado Lagoon, warm as bathwater; they biked the island's north coast, where patches of the ocean shone green; they ran past the low, sprawling citadel of Old San Juan. After two days of recovery, they paddled through the mangroves in the Bioluminescent Bay, slipped out of their kayaks, and floated on their backs, feeling oddly at home in the nighttime waters, which ran in neon rivulets down their arms when they reached for the sky. They hiked the El Yunque rainforest. Then they drove.

Eva wanted to see Cabo Rojo on the more remote southwestern coast. She'd read somewhere about red limestone cliffs, salt flats, fishing villages, a long, white beach. Delepine navigated using the crude half-page map from the rental car agency. It was an outline of the island with a few dots for cities. Cabo Rojo wasn't on it, but there was really only one main road to follow. They made a quick stop at Arecibo Observatory. The huge telescope dish, with its concrete towers and suspension cables, looked like a mammoth spider crawling out of the rainforest.

They kept driving. Two hours later, all Delepine knew was they had not yet reached the coast, nor the dot on their map marking the city of Mayaguez, just north of Cabo Rojo. On each turn, they wound deeper into a maze of narrowing streets. The concrete buildings drew closer together and some of them leaned on one another, grown weary. Balconies jutted into the street and looked as though they might drop. The streets became absurdly steep. Twice they scraped the underbelly of the car. As Eva inched downhill, riding the brakes, Delepine saw a spread of corrugated metal roofs with rust-eaten holes. She kept her finger on the dot for Mayaguez, as if she could prevent them from getting lost that way. With her free hand, she locked the doors.

Eva tried to gas up the next hill, but the car sputtered a third of the way up. Delepine scanned the street to see if they had attracted attention. Nothing moved in the streets, not even the litter that edged the sidewalk. They passed a fire hydrant that had been knocked on its side; the exposed ring at its base was hollow and bone dry. Beside it was an overturned bucket cracked nearly in half. Where were all the skeletal, slope-backed cats and dogs that stalked the rest of the island? Even a fluttering chicken would do. Four or five turns ago, she'd seen a gas station with abandoned pumps and a sign. *No hay gas.* Now she thought she saw movement near an archway that led to a crumbling set of steps.

Eva backed the car down the near-vertical hill and turned into an alley. A man walked in front of the car. Eva stepped on the brakes.

"Go around him," Delepine said.

"Are you crazy? There's no room."

The man was small, around sixty years of age, sun-browned and wearing a yellowed undershirt. He tapped on Eva's window. She rolled it down a few inches. He squinted into the car and looked at Eva, then Delepine, then the empty backseat. He had thick, peppery eyebrows and a mustache.

"Tan perdidas? A dónde van?" He waved his hand down the tight alley. As he turned, Delepine saw that he was holding a pistol behind his back.

"Cabo Rojo," Eva said.

He shook his head. "No lo conozco."

"Mayaguez?" Eva asked.

He shook his head again.

"He's got a gun," Delepine said. "What's he saying? He's got a gun." She looked up at the windows of the buildings. Did anyone know they were there? Two or three windows were boarded up. The ones on ground level were obscured by rusted bars.

A man—a boy, really, nineteen or twenty—was shuffling toward them in rubber slide sandals. One of his knees turned the wrong way and he dragged the foot on that side. He stopped beside Delepine's closed window and pounded on it. "Qué tenés ahí, mami?" He walked around the hood to Eva's side.

"Close that window," Delepine said.

But the boy was already reaching an arm in. It was hairless and sinewy. He pressed his shoulder into the window as he groped for the lock and then the handle.

The older man was yelling at him.

"Fuera de aquí, cabrón," Eva said, and shoved her purse into his dangling hand.

The boy was shaking the purse; he couldn't get it out. "Ábrete."

Eva lowered the window a few more inches. But the boy dropped the purse into Eva's lap and unlocked the door from the inside.

"I'm getting out," Eva said. Her voice was hoarse, as if she hadn't spoken all day.

"No," Delepine said. "Don't." What area was it where the locals ignored the stoplights because the carjacking had gotten so bad? But when Eva stepped out, Delepine did, too. Eva slipped around the back of the car to Delepine's side and grabbed her hand.

The man and the boy were arguing. The man took hold of the boy's ponytail and yanked it. The air was hot and still, but Delepine shivered. The hand that held Eva's was slippery wet. Which of them was sweating so much? Graffiti was thickly layered on the building facades. She tried to make out the scrawls. There were three red, slanted words at the bottom of one door. *El fin viene.* Near it was a painting of a blue rooster.

The boy made a sudden loping dash toward them. One of his rubber sandals snapped against the asphalt.

Now both the boy and the man were cackling. The boy had only feinted, and Delepine had dodged behind Eva. Had she really? Delepine was overcome with fear and humiliation.

The boy waggled his fingers at her. He was chattering nonstop; he was on a roll; she was good material. He threw an arm around Eva and let loose a phlegmy laugh. The man leaned on the car and grinned so hard his mustache was almost horizontal.

"Let's run," Delepine whispered into Eva's hair. "We have to run."

Eva turned to her, doubtful.

Delepine grabbed Eva's arm and pulled. "Come on!"

Eva cursed and pushed the boy away. The boy stumbled and laughed again.

For once, Delepine led. She ran back the way they had come, out of the alley, up a hill, down another hill, following the pitted road. She processed nothing, no sights or sounds. She was just trying not to trip. Eva was suddenly in front of her.

When they came upon the main road again, Eva squatted. Delepine lay down on the scratchy grass at the side of the road and curled up as small as she could. The sudden end to all that movement made her face throb. Things were still flying past her head. If she held her breath so her mind went silent, she could hear that boy's rattling laugh. He was

50 still laughing, she thought.

"Was that necessary?" Eva asked. "I was going to give them our cash."

When she no longer felt like throwing up, Delepine said, "They were dangerous."

"Okay then."

Delepine felt herself flushing. Eva was laughing at her, too. She turned over so that she was lying on her back. The clouds were clotting. The brightness of the sky burned her eyes. "What was he saying about me?"

Eva picked a short blade of grass. "Just the usual. Nothing interesting."

Delepine looked around. The road was more open here, but nothing felt safe. She wanted badly to be back in the hotel, making instant coffee, kicking off her shoes, crawling into bed with Eva, flipping channels, giggling at the telenovelas.

Eva sighed. "Do you remember how far we are from Arecibo? We can get help there."

"Forty, fifty miles?" Delepine was still lying on her back; it was hard to move. She followed a power line with her eyes. It ended in a tangle next to the pole.

Eva checked her watch. "Well, it's 11 a.m. We'd better start running." She stretched her left calf, then her right.

Because they wanted to reach Arecibo before dark, they kept up a demanding pace. Along the main road, the houses spread out. As they ran past the lush tropical vegetation and clotheslines and tarp-roofed carports, Delepine felt almost normal again. They were just running.

But she was not fully recovered from the race. Even though she'd spent twenty minutes in a tub of ice water and popped a handful of Advils. "Vitamin I," Eva called the pills. Now, just four days later, Delepine was running the longest distance of her life. And it was mountainous.

There was no food and no water. At one house, they stopped and drank from a hose in the yard. They crawled into a foresty stretch and peed; she thought she had to go, but only a trickle came out. "Ready?" Eva said. It was the only thing she had said for miles. Delepine nodded, and they started running again. She should not have stopped. Her feet would barely leave the ground.

She was wearing sneakers, khaki shorts, and a gray silk tank top darkened with sweat. Her clothes were too tight, and they stuck to her. She had nothing in her pockets. And nothing inside of her. She could not do it. She did not have it. Every part of her was soft, like she'd been deboned. She took a step forward and almost collapsed. Eva was seven, eight, nine steps beyond her.

"Wait," Delepine called.

Eva came back to her. Wasted steps.

"I need a second."

"Here," Eva said, guiding her to a clearing. Delepine sat down below a leafy tree. Vines were trying to strangle its trunk.

"Stay here, I'll keep going. We're close. Arecibo is close." Eva pointed down the road. "I remember that house with the silver truck. It won't be long from here."

"No. Just give me a second."

"I promise I won't be long."

"No, Eva. Just wait."

"Come on, you know you can't keep going like this."

"No, no. Can't you wait one second? Don't leave me here!" Delepine tried to push herself to a stand, but her arms gave out. She started dry heaving. A great sob filled her, and it leaked out in bits.

Eva shook her head. "I know, I know." But she did not. She would never know. "The sooner I go, the sooner I'll come back to get you." She rubbed Delepine's shoulder.

Eva walked out to the road, turned around, and waved. A gesture intended to reassure. It looked like a taunt. Eva ran. Her figure disappeared then reappeared in a bend. Even from a distance it was clear she was moving fast, her feet pushing hard off the ground.

Delepine sat with her back to the tree trunk. Its scales pricked her. She sat for hours, decades. She hadn't made it. When it counted. After all was said and done. Worse, she was a coward. Worse—alone. She shuddered, then sat very still. The sky darkened so slowly she felt it had always been like this, a dusky bolt of wool, unrolled over her head, the new moon an accidental cut.

Night.

A gray van from Arecibo Observatory pulled up. Eva helped her in. The driver, a man in a red baseball cap with the visor flipped up, nodded. "I wasn't sure you'd be there," he said and laughed. Eva passed back a bottle of water and a Styrofoam container of rice and beans, both of which Delepine finished before she even registered she was drinking or eating. She wanted more. She could not be filled up.

She lay out in the middle row. She didn't bother with the seatbelt and had to jam her foot against Eva's seat to keep from rolling off. It was dark and humid. It sounded like the air conditioning was on but didn't feel like it. The man was trying to make conversation with Eva. "This morning?" he asked. "You started running this morning?"

Eva asked about reporting a stolen car. Had it really been stolen? Delepine tried not to think too much about it.

No matter how her thoughts turned, she could feel a splinter lodged in there. She was safe. She didn't feel safe. She'd discovered something hard-edged, one post of a fence whose dimensions she didn't know.

The next morning, Delepine could not move.

"Jesus, I'm sore," Eva said, but she was already hopping around the hotel room, lining things up in her suitcase, checking their flight status.

On the phone, she tried to explain things to the car rental company. Judging by the length of the conversation, they gave her more trouble than the police had. Eva hung up and paused by the nightstand. "I slept like the dead."

Delepine looked at the digital alarm clock. She'd slept fourteen hours. But it was a sleep she remembered, a kind of surface sleep like a thin blanket you quivered beneath. The inside of her cheek was tender; she'd chewed her own flesh during the night. She sat up with immense effort. It was not soreness. Was it real damage? Where? She assessed her body. Everywhere.

Eva held out four brown ibuprofen tablets and a glass of water.

Delepine picked them out of Eva's palm one by one.

"You know what would help?" Eva grinned. "Get back out there. A quick recovery run. It'd be good before a long plane ride, don't you think?"

Delepine whipped the tablets at the wall. Hard, little flicks like gravel hitting a windshield.

"Jesus, Del. A joke."

After the Half Ironman, they planned to toss off a sprint triathlon. It was so easy they trained only once, on a short, hilly ride. Eva pedaled like a lunatic and left Delepine gasping in her wake. She had to wonder if Eva had been holding back these last fifteen years, not within her reach at all.

In the first segment of the tri, a dinky half-mile swim, Delepine paused and looked for the first buoy. She treaded water. If she stopped moving, she would sink to the dark bottom. The inflated orange pyramid was far—farther than she could make it. She was kicked several times, not hard. Brushed by gentle hands. The swimmers hadn't yet spread out. She found herself coughing and flagging down a rescue boat.

The rescuer, a bearded man with pale blue eyes, pulled her out by the armpits. She scrambled in, clumsy, sticking her rear end in the air, rocking the boat so the man had to put his hands out for balance and say, "Whoa."

He told her to exhale. "Let it out slow." He smiled. "Don't be embarrassed. This happens to lots of first-timers. You're not the only one."

Disqualified, Delepine watched the race from a grassy hill. Many athletes had scrawled their ages on their arms or legs in permanent marker. She watched an older woman tear past a pair of twenty-somethings, the black "65" on her calf a little banner of glory.

Around the time of Hippie's birth, the economic downturn nearly halved Delepine and Rodney's savings. Six years later, the housing market that had danced at their fingertips for so long suddenly shot out of reach. Engineers that looked like teenagers snatched up the condos they'd been saving for. They gave up trying to buy; they were in their mid-fifties—past pretending. They rented a tiny apartment in San Francisco, in the Outer Richmond. It brought beach walks and daily views of gray sky over gray water. It was cold through all seasons. The wind was harsh and wet, and Delepine could feel it inside the house, wearing away at the wood and paint. The draft slunk around and found her.

For temporary warmth, she locked herself in the tiny bathroom and ran hot water into the deep, footed tub. The book-sized skylight and the mirror over the pedestal sink fogged up. The bathroom was too small for cabinets or vanities, and there was only a stack of worn towels on a wooden chair. On the ledge above the tub were a jar of bath salts, bar soap, shampoo.

Steam hovered just over the surface of the filled tub. In the old house, the hot water came out nearly boiling, and afterward the copper spouts were scalding. Delepine eased into the water. Her body had settled into the shape it had been trying to become all this time: thick and soft at the middle, dense and sturdy everywhere else. She dug her thumbs into the soles of her curved feet. She could no longer wear heels at work. She thought of days when she used to swim in the frigid ocean. Afterward it was important to take a lukewarm soak, not to shock the system, to bring the body temperature back up in increments. Now her late afternoon baths were immoderately hot. That feeling of sweating in the sun with a pounding face, of chugging up a dry, treeless hill. Every cell of her body tried to retain that sensation of fire. So she could walk around the house afterward, feeling that the draft of sea air was a pleasant breeze. So the world was refreshing again. Her skin was rasp-dry.

She could not stop drinking cups after cups of hot tea. How else to warm the inside of her? Three years earlier, Rodney had been diagnosed with oral cancer. After a brief remission, it came back. It was no use asking how it had come to this. He didn't chew tobacco or smoke. One doctor said the hot coffee might have been a contributing factor. Inconclusive studies and such. Anyway, it was time for a difficult decision. He was sorry to have to ask this. Did he want a glossectomy?

"Excuse me?"

"The removal of the tongue."

Delepine thought, I haven't talked to him enough.

After the surgery, Rodney retired early and took to spending summers in Washington. He stayed in an old family cabin and worked on restoring it. He'd always wanted a place of his own. There was little left of the town Rodney had grown up in, just an abandoned paper mill factory, some razed houses, a cemetery, a post office. Mostly he stayed in. He fixed the roof and replaced the windows. He filled the insect holes in the wooden walls with borate plugs. Using a manual coffee grinder and an old kettle, he steeped the grounds of his coffee in a tin cup until the coffee turned to slime. He didn't drink much of it, just breathed in its fumes. He read his sci-fi books by oil lamp. Sometimes Delepine visited him for a week or two. She chattered while he nodded or didn't nod. She was charmed by his home. They made love on a cot that started by the wall and ended two feet away. All night long, she pointed her feet and curled her toes as she slept. She couldn't get rid of some kind of tension pulling her taut. When she woke, she tongued the raw insides of her cheeks.

But mostly she left Rodney alone for the summers, free to explore his other life.

A few times a year, she saw Eva, who still wore tight jeans and sneakers and looked like she still trained. Did she? Delepine did not ask, and Eva did not tell her. The last time she'd visited had been for Hippie's sixteenth birthday. She'd brought along a card with a hot air balloon on the front, and tucked a crisp hundred-dollar bill inside. Eva showed her Hippie's new car, a BMW from his father, who was taking him to Spain that summer. Barcelona? Madrid? No, Granada. Delepine did not ask where that was. She had been two and a half loops around the equator, but really, she'd been nowhere. Hippie looked at the envelope and told her he preferred to be called Hyde. He opened the card in front of her and glanced at the handwriting, too briefly to have read it, she thought, or maybe this generation could insta-scan. He thanked her and shoved the bill into his back pocket, as though it were a five or ten. His friend appeared, and the two of them shuffled inside. Through the open window, she heard them saying, "I hope your birthday has you flying high." "I hope *your* birthday has you flying high." "I hope your birthday has you flying *high.*" Reciting the printed message inside her card.

Eva called him back out to say goodbye. Delepine stared hard at him, trying to get him to lift his sleepy, withdrawn eyes so she could peer into them. He wore a beanie, though the temperature was in the

eighties. His lashes fluttered as though this sweet patch of yard in
partial shade was too bright for him. He was so pale; he lived indoors.
Hyde, Hyperion, Hippie. Look *up*. Didn't he remember he'd once loved
her beyond all earthly, expressible love? ✄

Chia-Chia Lin is the author of the novel The Unpassing *(Farrar, Straus & Giroux), and lives in San Bruno, California.*

HANGOVER 1.1.2019

SAM SAX

Like a hammer swung into antique champagne flutes

Like a family heirloom traded for a Twix

Like a red dictionary dropped from a replica famous bridge

Like a robe made out of skin that, turns out, is your skin & oops you must wear it

Like the man who lives in your occipital lobe slowly whittles a sad stick and sighs

Like a headwrap made of crane flies

Like a framed section of your brain hanged in a museum

Like a school of hungry kids all banging their forks & knives at once

Maybe that's all a bit much

All i'm trying to say is last night i drank

Attempting to celebrate the end of a terrible year

In preparation for an even worse one

& despite the coming & current devastations

The private & public executions of the soul

The laws passed to unstitch the eyes from camera phones

—still we managed to assemble some friends

to drink clear liquors & eat factoried chickens.

& a part of me loves it, this morning

how this is a pain of my own making

this throb—a diamond lodged in my head

ODE TO THE YOUNG QUEER HOLDING A PLANT ON THE TRAIN

SAM SAX

it was a hard year already. the world collapsing in predictable ways.
i was on my way across town to reconcile with an ex who'd done me
dirty & was busy warding off the panic gathered up in my ribs like
the limbs of a broken umbrella when the train dipped underground

at macarthur & there you were—sitting across from me holding
in your lap a small split-leafed philodendron & it was as if i hadn't looked
upon another living thing in years. below the earth, inside this thin
living room lit by liquified fossils. ruffled green evening gown fanning out

between your black acrylics. opening as if to mock the light streaming
from our phones. down here in the tunnels where life don't go. in tunnels
carved by men's exploited fingers. down here where there was no light
until we decided to be the lord our-selves & say let there be

this bitch, holding a small ceramic planet in your hands, the whole
damned earth. & all us on it who've been defiled by agronomy & smoke,
are now opening and broad of frond along with you. we living where
we do not belong. both invasive and made to uproot. deserving

blame. without country. seeds sown into the hems of our skirts.
today i read & was prepared for so much suffering. to see the man
who hurt me bad enough i only fed on dirty light. but then you arrived
like a child holding fire & not the other way around.

o plant child, singing a little song into the breathing green blades.
i hope you survive us. us filled to the brim with micro-fauna listening

60 to our own poison root music. my man and i survived each other
despite our best efforts. the earth will survive us the same

& all the plants will bow their heads out of respect each time the sun
sets and that, my dear, will have to be acknowledgment enough.

sam sax is a Wallace Stegner Fellow at Stanford University and the author of Bury It *(Wesleyan University Press), winner of the James Laughlin Award, and lives in Oakland.*

UNSENTIMENTAL EDUCATION

**LEARNING THE LITERARY ROPES WHEN THE
WORLD, AND THE WRITER, WERE YOUNG.**

PAUL WILNER

Everything we do now is most likely something we've done before and will almost certainly repeat.

Where id was, ego shall be, as the (currently unfashionable) Sigmund put it. The illusion that any of us are different, in any essential respect, from the squalling infants who left our mothers' wombs, is a category error—a particularly Western, even more *Californian*, form of post-Enlightenment wish fulfillment. Hindsight may be 20/20, but it's an arbitrary construct, a way to make sense of what we didn't understand then in the light of what we don't know and likely never will.

Looking back at my life as a teenager, arriving in San Francisco from New York in the mid-'60s just as the acid was hitting the fan was a change in emotional, as well as physical, temperature.

Like most (or like many) kids, I was inherently resistant to change, and was initially put off by the sheer Californian healthiness and Archie-Andrews-and-Betty-Cooper-in-Riverdale of it all: *so many blonde people! surfers!*

And Lowell High School, way out in the fog of the Sunset district, near Stonestown and San Francisco State, was considerably different from Horace Mann, the prep school I'd attended the previous year as

62 part of a brief familial adventure in upward mobility—let alone J.H.S. 52, the Inwood public junior high I'd gone to before that. (Kareem Abdul-Jabbar, known in those days as Lew Alcindor, lived in the Dyckman Street housing projects in the neighborhood, and we'd sometimes see him hanging out, looking gangly on the concrete public basketball courts, or towering over the crowd at the local library.)

Lowell was the "academic" high school, the S.F. equivalent to Bronx Science or Stuyvesant, where a high-achieving mix of largely Jewish and Asian American kids gathered to compete. But it seemed considerably more low-key to me, at least by East Coast standards, as I tried to adjust.

After a brief respite in Sausalito's Hurricane Gulch, my folks, who were inveterate city dwellers, took a flat on Franklin Avenue, between Broadway and Pacific. I rode the 47 Van Ness bus down to Market Street, then transferred to the crowded Muni M line to get to Lowell. It was a parallel (though considerably different) experience to riding the subways in New York, freezing in the winter and overwhelmed by sweaty citizens in the summer, with Miss Rheingold advertisements above the graffiti-tagged windows.

I was disoriented, jolted out of my comfort zone, though trying to fit in with the rich kids at Horace Mann, with their parents' fancy apartments on the Upper East Side, had been an uncomfortable fit as well. Jack Kerouac had attended the school on a football scholarship, too, and William Carlos Williams before him, but poets were by no means the alumni most celebrated by these Ivy League strivers, destined for futures at Harvard or Yale, then Wall Street or D.C. Getting into Columbia or Cornell was considered déclassé in comparison.

But I quickly discovered that, first impressions notwithstanding, gnarly surfers by no means dominated my new surroundings. It turned out that Lowell had a sizable Boho contingent, as I found when one of the first girls I met at school handed me a button with the legend

"Psychedelicize suburbia." This after I established my cred by telling her I'd attended one of the first anti-Vietnam protests in Washington D.C. the year before.

Drug culture was just hitting the scene, though I was only dipping my finger in stems, seeds, and the "matchboxes" where the weed was then stashed, before it graduated to lids, let alone bales.

I struck up a friendship with a longhaired pal named John (last name omitted to protect the innocent). A Presidio Heights kid, his parents hosted chamber music concerts in their well-appointed living room, with original art work by Paul Klee and the like hanging in their halls. It was a far cry from what I was accustomed to in the middle-class apartments of Washington Heights.

Fitzgerald was right—the rich *are* different from you and me—so it's probably needless to say that John was sometimes angry and confused as we negotiated our way through our respective post-puberty rites. But as a quintessential "good boy," I got a kick out of those who felt the freedom to act out. And his sardonic wit kept the problems we inevitably faced in unsentimental perspective.

After settling in, I recruited John as co-editor of the school literary magazine: I never liked the loneliness, let alone responsibility, of steering the ship as a solo pilot.

We called it *Wonderful*, from *As You Like It*: "*O wonderful, wonderful, and most wonderful wonderful! And yet again, wonderful, and after that, out of all hooping.*"

We probably could have used a little more hooping and a lot less wonder, but we balanced the flower child dippiness with a Dylan quote: "Anyone who's ever slept in the back seat of a car knows that I'm just not a schoolteacher."

We didn't really have meetings for the magazine; neither of us liked the formality of such gatherings and were too full of ourselves to

64 welcome much dialogue. But nevertheless, we soon gathered a formidable group of talented soon-to-be's.

Like Jessica Hagedorn, a budding Filipino American poet. Long before she rose to fame with *Dogeaters* and other works of biting wit and barbed politics, Jessica wore a black leather jacket and her boyfriend rode a menacing motorcycle—even then, she was not someone to be messed with lightly.

Her poem "Love Song" was sexy, smart, and filled with adolescent angst:

> *The first time i died*
> *I cried*
> *inside.   but*
> *the music was too good*
> *not to hear again*
> *so*
> *   i fled*
> *from the dead   and*
> *the second time   death*
> *came to me*
> *i could see*
> *your realness and flesh*
> *taste*
> *bitter saliva kisses*
> *O*
> *your anger was too good*
> *not to hear again*
> *so*
> *   i reconsidered fakery*
> *yours*
> *and mine and all*

the writhing corpses and
gods;
Boys and girls in
their desperate silks and
fluid contortions

Jessica's polar opposite, Carol Snow, a preternaturally quiet girl from Diamond Heights with a gift for Dickinsonian tart remarks, offered a gnomic prose poem:

> *As if you were there, and I were here, and you were to receive a*
> *sacred epistle, written even late at night, with a song that remains*
> *a secret in the back, and mother in the front, and someone else as*
> *well, here. As if you were someone who receives sacred epistles,*
> *and one who receives yea, even privileged glimpses into you know,*
> *heart. This is not one, but as if you did, as if you were a bearded*
> *minded cripple, or a man who teaches by day, or plays at it, and*
> *goes home to smoke a cigar. As if you were someone like a Beatle,*
> *who keeps getting hearts and minds on your birthday, as gifts*
> *you know, and cards drowned in love. As if you were someone*
> *I didn't know.*
>
> *Dear Sir.*

After matriculating at Cal, where she was mentored by Robert Hass, Carol became a recognized poet, with haiku-like work capturing moments recollected in tranquility with emotion rippling beneath the surface.

Russell Leong, the son of a Chinatown newspaperman, offered tough, taut images, accompanied by his own art work. (Russell later wrote several volumes of well-received fiction, memoir, poetry, and art work and served as the longtime editor of UCLA's *Amerasia Journal*).

Here's what he offered us:

I paint an ordinary face
of dabs of dark oil
and dull eyes swept
beneath chalk circles.
Shivering holes of nostril
and clenched mouth of red-pink
holding a smearful of sensations.

Jeff Sheppard, a quiet soul, surfaced with this Brautigan-esque title: "I'm putting you down, Bill, forgive me." Jeff was later befriended by the mustachioed Trout Fisher, who dedicated a poem to him on the perils and fleeting pleasures of fame: "Hey! This Is What It's All About."

Not bad for kids starting out.

We were lucky then, luckier than we knew.

The Beats' wild and woolly contributions to the San Francisco scene had come a little before us, but the liberating spirit of their work, shattering norms of sexuality and self-expression, was still very much in the air.

Haight-Ashbury goddess Lenore Kandel's ecstatic *The Love Book*, a compilation of "holy erotica," had just been busted for obscenity. Lew Welch, a wryer, more intoxicated version of Gary Snyder, was also a strong presence, along with perennial playwright, poet, and lady's man Michael McClure. (A production of McClure's play *The Beard* would also get busted for its final scene of simulated cunnilingus between Billy the Kid and Jean Harlow in an imagined close encounter.)

Sometimes at night we'd venture out to salons like the I/Thou Coffee Shop in the Haight, where you'd see the be-caped underground filmmaker, Satanist, and poet Kenneth Anger surface for sulfurous readings, or hang out at Gino & Carlo's in North Beach, where the hippies, Beats, and local drunks met in harmonic convergence.

Our school literary club invited the poet Stan Rice, an S.F. State teacher who was married to Anne Rice, of subsequent vampiric fame, to Lowell for a talk. When we adjourned to the courtyard for fresh air and some smokes (nothing illegal, surprisingly enough), we were descended upon by the school *gendarmes*. Nothing serious ensued, luckily, although I think Anne Wallach, the adviser to the literary magazine, may have intervened with Harry Krytzer, the sometimes truculent Dean of Boys.

Mrs. Wallach was the spiritual leader of Lowell's all-star English Department, providing encouragement and firm boundaries in equal measure. (Her sister was the iconic *New Yorker* magazine film critic Pauline Kael; they were brought up amidst the community of Jewish American Socialist chicken ranchers who thrived for a time in Petaluma, though Pauline made the escape back East after making her bones as a caustic critic on KPFA).

Although her style was quieter, Mrs. Wallach's acumen was not to be discounted, either. She also ran interference with me in a later dispute with Krytzer—I forget the exact nature of the offense but do recall his telling me he thought I was "a good example of the kind of student who came out here from New York." Thanks, bro.

It was a great, eye-opening adventure, but my style, then and now, has been to stay on the fringes, not the landing point, of any scene, however loosely defined. Working as a journalist, my trade for the last three-odd decades, is by definition the stance of an observer, not a direct participant.

And the scene was splintering, as the cosmic eye of mass media—prefiguring the current onslaught of technological omnipresence—distorted and changed something that, at its source, aimed for and sometimes achieved Edenic purity and sweetness.

In a larger sense, the mad refraction was embodied by Ken Kesey's public flight from literature, where he had made his bones with *One Flew Over the Cuckoo's Nest* and *Sometimes a Great Notion*, the latter a less celebrated but more deeply novelistic exploration of his blue-collar roots in Oregon. He'd transformed into a psychedelic ranger, intent on going ever further into the abyss, surrounded by worshippers falling for his macho mystique. This is the scene that was deconstructed by Tom Wolfe in *The Electric Kool-Aid Test*, and, for that matter, Joan Didion's *Slouching Towards Bethlehem*, which casts a cold eye on the street people of the Haight, hanging on to this day in a vain attempt to summon a past that never was.

The beating heart of wild rock 'n' roll that began with a San Francisco Mime Troupe benefit organized by their then-publicist, Bill Graham, and was carried on by Bill's unruly counterparts, The Family Dog (group motto: "May the baby Jesus shut your mouth and open your mind"), was turned into a cash machine, as the inevitable capitalist wheels kicked in.

As for us, who were there then, well, we did what we could. And moved on.

Our loosely gathered group of young *littérateurs* hasn't stayed in significant touch. I think we have a sense, however tacit, that we owed it to each other to allow each of us to grow up in our own way, assuming we somehow survived the struggles of the time. We respected each other's right to walk our own road.

The convergence may not have always been harmonic, but in a time when everything feels up for grabs—I know that's every time, but perhaps even more so now—it's heartening to remember where we were, as well as where we may be going.

Life and literature, in whatever order you choose to put them, were there for the taking. I believed that then, and believe that now.

School's out, but we're still here. Forever. ❧

Paul Wilner is a poet, critic, and freelance journalist and a frequent contributor to ZYZZYVA.

OPENING THE MAIL

W.S. DI PIERO

The notices hit my inbox once a week, it seems,
dusty phantasmal names sickly and unwanted.
I don't remember them, the boys from my high school,
their Irish, Slavic, Italian names in the "subject" line,
put there by Principle Father Rich, once one of us,
we tough tender souls weathering snotty skies.
The announcements come like rude enchantments, a sullen choir
beseeching with their newly minted news. They were there,
as I was, but the names are husks, blowing through time,
boys I never knew: Charlie McNally, Cosimo Picucci,
Stosh Grzywinski, the Two-Streeters and corner boys,
vets, mummers, contractors, bankers, teachers, priests,
returning to their place among the infinite
unheard-from dead. The e-mails remind me of the skulls
the old and new painters place just so, on a bright, rucked,
disheveled tablecloth, or scabbed rickety stool
impoverished in the studio, reminding us
of the weighty skulls we hold of children and lovers at night,
in bed, to keep them close and tell them that we're here.

THE SMELTERS

W.S. DI PIERO

The Alleghenies (*clack!*) preserve
cries of the early peoples, settlers,

ironmasters who hauled hundreds
of wagons of harvested trees,

in the dark of early day, like now,
our black and white fall world,

and cooked ore inside these silenced
stone-stack blast furnaces:

their smoke choked everybody
and charcoaled the sunny air.

Deep inside the thinned-out forest,
a sanctuary houses other cries:

healing or retired or hospice
falcons, hawks, eagles, owls.

I get close to their shadowed quiet.
The woods (*clack!*) look like gangs

of gaunt, coltish boys. The fires gulped
the heavy pine woods Shawnee hunted.

In our early iron-desk schoolrooms,
grinning Sacred Heart sisters smacked

pine rulers on bad boys' thighs.
They groaned, they bawled to be let free.

Power takes its pleasure where it will.
I watch the captive raptors pressed into

the cage's fibrous dark. I watch
as if they could deliver us. I am

the useless sentimentalist:
no metaphor changes time, its teeth.

Market forces sicken tribe
and polity. One bird reminds us.

O mother. *Clack!* O great-horned owl.
Sound the alarm. The killer's here.

The killer is me. Your beak (*Clack!*) breaks
inside my ear. Warn me of me.

Simone Di Piero's most recent poetry collection is The Complaints (Carnegie Mellon) *and his most recent prose book is* Mickey Rourke and the Bluebird of Happiness: A Poet's Notebooks *(Carnegie Mellon). He lives in San Francisco.*

ANDI TAYLOR VS. ARTEMIS VICTOR

RITA BULLWINKEL

Andi Taylor is pumping her hands together, hitting her own flat stomach, thinking not of her mother sitting at home with her little brother, not of her car, which barely got her here, not of her summer job, her lifeguarding at the overcrowded community pool, not of the four-year-old she watched die, the four-year-old she practically killed, and his blue cheeks. They shouldn't give teenagers the job of saving children. It doesn't matter how many CPR classes you've taken. She killed the boy with her wandering eyes. His swimsuit had small red trucks on it. He looked like he was made out of the plastic. The feel of his thigh when she pulled him from the bottom of the pool, already dead, and the way it was so easy to grip, because it was so small, she's not thinking about it. She's looking at the skylight and the light it's letting in on this shit-hole gym and she's thinking about the things she always does wrong when she fights, her lazy left guard, the way her left hand slips away and doesn't protect her face if she's not thinking about it. She is also thinking about the way Artemis Victor will get her. If Andi Taylor doesn't think about this, this fight will be over in a matter of seconds. Andi Taylor needs to think about her spacing and her stomach. Andi Taylor needs to think about her stance.

They're still sitting and looking at each other meanly. They know each other but have never fought before. When you join the women's youth boxing league, this facade of a sports association makes you pay $200 and then you get a free subscription to their magazine, which profiles its members, young girl boxers, one by one, so you see who's out there, even if they are across the country, and you get a good sense of who you're up against, and you know who they've fought and who they are going to fight and what their favorite hobby is because god only knows what kind of a journalist writes this excuse for a magazine, but whoever it is seems to think that it is valuable profile information and that it should be included in every athlete profile, because in every issue there it is: name, hometown, favorite color, hobby, wins and losses, photo of the girl in gloves. The photo is a wildcard because some girls choose to take it in their gym clothes, while others choose to take it in halter tops, their hair down, their head tilted and their gloves resting on their hips.

Andi Taylor would know Artemis Victor anywhere because Artemis Victor is the youngest of the three Victor sisters, a family of boxers whose parents come to every single one of Artemis's matches with shirts that say "Victor," which is, of course, ridiculous, their proclamation of their daughters' winning records on their chests.

Everyone knows the Victor sisters and what they've won and what they've lost, and the judges treat Artemis's family like old friends, which in boxing is especially infuriating because the gray area of a call is often so present, and if you know a judge has a special relationship with the participants, you can't help thinking, I'm being slighted, this is the end of me, if only I had parents willing to befriend my coaches, if only I had parents that could get off work, that didn't work, that could come see me win.

Mr. and Mrs. Victor sit in folding chairs next to the ring. There are nine other onlookers: other girl fighters, a journalist from the local paper, and Bob, the owner of this gym.

Artemis Victor is rolling her shoulders. She's looking at Andi Taylor and thinking, You are ugly. I am prettier than you and I am going to beat you, too.

Artemis Victor thinks about being prettier than Andi Taylor, because she knows, somewhere inside her, that no one cares who wins this match, that who is prettier matters more to the world around her, that who is more attractive, or more seductive, has more power out in the world outside this gym. Artemis sizes up other women physically everywhere. I'm the prettiest woman in this room, she thinks. There's one woman, over there, who may be prettier, if you like girls that look like drug addicts. There are men that like girls who look like drug addicts. When Artemis Victor thinks of herself in the future, she thinks of herself as wildly successful in a big house, maybe in Miami, not a drug addict. Artemis has never been to Miami. Artemis Victor has a teddy bear that has a doll's shirt that says "Victor."

"That's my girl!" yells Mrs. Victor.

✳ ✳ ✳

Artemis Victor always thinks she is going to win. It's not a bad habit to get in. If one has that gene, where self-doubt can be thrown out of the window, it can be beneficial to employ. Artemis Victor hates her oldest sister. Her oldest sister won the Daughters of America Cup four years ago. Her middle sister got a silver. Even if Artemis wins the whole thing, wins the whole tournament and becomes the best in the world, the best woman under eighteen in the world at boxing, she'll still be second best to her oldest sister, Star Victor, because Star became the best in the world before her and is now married with a husband and a child and well on her way to owning a house if not being rich.

✳ ✳ ✳

ANDI TAYLOR VS. ARTEMIS VICTOR

Artemis Victor has no idea what it takes to own a house, but she knows what it takes to beat other people, which is what owning property seems like, beating other people at owning a piece of the earth and making that piece of earth yours, not to be shared with other people, because the owning of the property is a product of your victory over other humans, as in, you won more dollars than them so now this slice of land is yours for keeps.

✿   ✿   ✿

It's not that Artemis Victor is stupid. She'd make an excellent banker, though she'll become a wine distributor. It's just that her values are very narrow. She has an insanely good eye for reading people, for knowing what they are thinking under the words they are speaking, for watching how people hold themselves when they talk to you, whether or not they are interested in you. She knows which of her high school teachers to feel bad for: the ones whose eyes dart around looking for someone to listen to them. She knows the right way to say a thing to make people think she is interested in hearing them speak.

Artemis Victor is also a vegan. She genuinely feels bad for animals. This was part of her profile in the Women's Youth Boxing Association magazine (the WYBA). Artemis Victor loves animals. She watched a documentary on the abuse of whales in theme parks and also thinks they should be let free.

✿   ✿   ✿

The referee is in the middle of the ring and is saying things to the girls about rules that they already know and have heard a hundred times before. They nod their heads and get up off their stools and begin to bounce up and down. Andi is bouncing much more than Artemis. Artemis paces forward, steady. They're both wearing silk shorts and tank tops. The elastic on their waistbands makes dents in their skin that will last for hours after they take their shorts off.

A week ago, Andi came home and took off her shorts and looked at the red ring of gulleys the shorts had left on her stomach. She fingered the indentation with her hands. When the marks disappeared an hour later, she was sad to not have them. They seemed like evidence of the work she'd done. She wished she had a black eye from a winning fight to wear around, to show people she was fighting, to show people her body was doing something that was hard.

✿　✿　✿

Andi's knee is out too far and Artemis moves in to force Andi to retract it back under her hips. These are the size-up seconds—the moments a fighter has to decide if and where their opponent has weaknesses.

If Artemis has a weakness, it is in the fact that she is a legacy. Her sisters' wins hang over her. She is reminded of them constantly. This is the tournament where she can be as good as her eldest sister, or the worst boxer in their family. The type of legacy that is the Victor family is rarer in boxing than other kinds of sports, but not unheard of. Youth women's boxing is a world small enough that the Victors could conquer it.

✿　✿　✿

Andi Taylor's knee is still not in the right place. Artemis lifts her lip up to her nose to show her red-mouth-guard-covered teeth.

✿　✿　✿

Artemis's biceps are balls of muscle. She can hit things harder than most people could throw a ball. Her back muscles are arched in two small hills on either side of her neck. Artemis begins to see a weakness in the way Andi moves where Artemis thinks she can place a hit. Artemis Victor thinks she can touch Andi Taylor. Just as Artemis thinks this, Andi hits the left side of Artemis Victor's ribs.

It's a hard blow that the judges call a hit immediately. The score is yelled loud enough so everyone can hear it. This is a point-hitting game, after all. That's why they wear padded headgear that circles their ears and cheeks and foreheads and buckles under their chins. This is target practice.

Andi had seen a tunnel of a vacancy between her right fist and Artemis's left ribcage. It had looked illuminated, like it was just begging to be filled with Andi's fist. Andi had put her hand in the hole to Artemis's body, that tunnel of vacancy, and then was filling the hole again, and again, until the referee got between them.

✿ ✿ ✿

The referee had checked the inside of Andi's gloves before he taped them onto her wrists. He was checking to see if she had put lead in them.

✿ ✿ ✿

They always do this before a match. It's part of the rules of the association.

✿ ✿ ✿

Andi loves when the referees reach into her gloves. She likes watching their hands go into a hole where her hands are about to go. The fact that they check every time makes Andi feel like she is capable of murder. Maybe she could put a rock in there. Maybe she is capable of killing the girl she is fighting. Every time the referees look in her gloves it is like they are saying, you are capable of killing, which feels good to Andi. Most people in her life don't seem to believe she is capable of anything, let alone killing someone with purpose, and with the wandering-eyes murder of the little boy, she wonders if she is also capable of killing someone with her fists.

※　※　※

To be clear, Andi never came close to putting anything in her gloves, not only because the referee surely would have found it, but because she didn't want the feeling of actually killing someone; she already had that. She wanted the feeling of someone thinking she was capable of the killing, which is exactly what the referees give her just by looking in her gloves before every match.

※　※　※

The boy with the red-truck shorts, Andi wasn't thinking about him, was not even the worst thing that had happened to Andi, or the first dead body she had seen. But, it was the smallest (the other dead body had been her father's). The smallness of the dead boy had seemed especially disgusting. The day had been so clear and dry. She hadn't cried. She vomited after it was clear that the red-truck kid was not going to come back to life. The vomiting made Andi feel like she herself was a child. She was surprised by her body's visceral repulsion to the dead red-truck kid. It was the image of his small, corn-dog-sized thigh that made her vomit. Andi hit Artemis again, this time on Artemis's shoulder. How long could she get away with hitting Artemis Victor?

※　※　※

Bob's Boxing Palace had been selected for the Daughters of America Cup because of its central location, the fact that it was vaguely in the middle of the American heartland, or was, at least, not near an ocean, and because Bob was the brother of the head of the Women's Youth Boxing Association, which collected $100 from each entrant to pay the referees, the judges, and the facility fees and the association officials for their time.

✿   ✿   ✿

Andi had used her lifeguarding money to pay the entry fee, which now seemed like blood money.

✿   ✿   ✿

There was always a qualifying, regional Daughters of America Cup, before the national one, so the WYBA collected fees from over one thousand women, which means that they did make a profit, usually fifty or sixty thousand dollars, and Bob got to take some of that home for having it at his beat gym.

✿   ✿   ✿

The difference between Artemis Victor and Andi Taylor's bodies was that Artemis was thicker. The muscles stuck out from her arms and her back like there were things under her skin. In Artemis's forearms there were clear lines of sinew from her wrists to her elbows. Her shoulders were broad, and looked especially large when she crammed them into strapless dresses. During fights she always wore make-up. Artemis wore waterproof mascara and a red stain on her lips.

✿   ✿   ✿

Andi was tall and gangly. She had a cross-country runner's body. People were always telling her she should try running long distances. She wasn't interested.

✿   ✿   ✿

In the hair arena, Artemis Victor had the archetype of a ponytail.

She had so much brown hair it barely fit in one rubber band. When she wasn't fighting, she wore it either on the side or in a big bun on top of her head. Even up, it was still long enough to brush against her shoulders. She always said she was growing it out to cut off and give to a girl with cancer, but she never cut her hair except in small, two- or three-inch trims.

✿ ✿ ✿

Andi Taylor's hair was so thin that when she braided the whole of it, the braid was as thin as one of her fingers. When her hair got wet, it felt slimy. Andi Taylor worried about her hair breaking off when it was really cold out. It had happened once, just with a couple pieces, but she had so little hair that it felt very dramatic, like she had lost something she had very little of and would never get back.

✿ ✿ ✿

The fact of the two girls' bodies was not lost on Artemis Victor or Andi Taylor or on any of the young women in the Daughters of America tournament. Their body was the only tool they had at their disposal. This wasn't lacrosse or tennis. There were no rackets. They had their arms and their legs and their headgear-clad heads and their glove-covered hands, although the gloves and the headgear were just there as a protective measure, to make sure they didn't kill each other. The gloves and the headgear weren't something they needed to perform the skill they had practiced, though they did, in their separate states, in their separate gyms, all practice with gloves and headgear. The gloves and the headgear were like clothing. One could box with them, or without them, just as one could, technically, swim naked or in a suit.

✿ ✿ ✿

ANDI TAYLOR VS. ARTEMIS VICTOR

Andi Taylor and Artemis Victor looked at each other's bodies under the roof of Bob's Boxing Palace and tried to figure out how they could make their fists touch each other's faces. This was the first match of the tournament, the semifinalist round. If you lost, you were out. There was no back door in the Daughters of America. ✂

Rita Bullwinkel is the author of the story collection Belly Up *(A Strange Object), and lives in San Francisco.*

CHANNEL 4

MICHAEL SEARS

A s a child I would wait for the afternoons that my mother would spend up in her bed, tired (as my father called it), to creep into the living room, mute the volume and turn the TV to Channel 4. I had first known that channel as an uncertain blackness that my father and I would visit on the nights he and I watched movies, and which would, since the input for the VCR ran through it, abruptly detonate into a static that, as if a violence done to the otherwise sequential logic of our cable package, vexed my father immensely. My father, who never disciplined me, never screamed nor used force, had always become terribly upset over minor events, and would grow disconsolate over clumsily dropped pieces of china, asking everyone in the house about fingerprints on the brass light-switch plates he'd installed in the living room and that frequently paused him with a presentation of his own image, miniaturized, and slightly warped by the indentation of the screws. After he returned from a business trip to India, he would, for years, over and over tell reluctantly obliging relatives and coworkers and acquaintances the story of how, on his first night staying at the Grand New Delhi, he had discovered that the reading light over his bed didn't work, and when he had gone to the front desk to let the manager know, the manager had told him, rather cheerfully, that he could find a light bulb for himself, down the street, at the outdoor market. At this point in the story, my father would pause to look from face to coldly bemused face, his own expression so terrifically unguarded, so naively betrayed, that, later in life, I'd have to look away during the telling to save him from a second betrayal. Even as a child, I was careful to diminish with feigned inattention the scope of the treachery worked upon my father by Channel 4 when, with bitterness, he was forced to mute the volume before he typed in the channel number, and then, as soon as the VCR had turned on—me motionless as when he negotiated a particularly difficult turn on a road—to unmute it.

It was during these interims of static that my father so indignantly suffered that I discovered that images, desultory and faint and scrambled, would, every now and again, make their way through Channel 4. Abruptly the static would clarify—as in a vision, there was a context-less glimpse of a man talking (muted), the colors of his body, along with those of the ground and sky, inverted. But the image would quickly vanish from the screen in a blizzard of visual noise, and from my memory soon after, too. For in the same way those inchoate thoughts that occur outside of words, on the peripheries of sleep, are dispersed by the intrusion of known and named phenomena (say, a car alarm going off in the night), those hazy images would dissolve from both the screen and my thoughts as soon as the trailers started. And what made what arose on Channel 4 further unclear was that my father didn't comment on it, nor did his face report seeing anything. It was as if I had hallucinated in a mild and forgivable way.

One night, as we were getting ready to watch *Jurassic Park*, the screen, down which white horizontal lines had been idly scrolling, all at once blinked to the image of a woman at the top of a staircase. It was only after the image vanished and the VCR turned on and the walls blushed with the red glow of the FBI warning against pirating that I realized she'd been wearing a robe, which she'd let drop. I did not, though, recognize the type of underwear she'd worn beneath or even that it was, in fact, underwear she was wearing. Like the intricacies of rhyme and meter in the poems my mother sometimes read me on the days she was feeling well, the complex interaction of straps and buckles she wore oppressed me with a feeling that was opaque and slippery and near holy in how far beyond my understanding it seemed, and perhaps for that reason impressed itself so powerfully upon me that I was, in that moment, ready to dedicate the rest of my life to deciphering it.

But I could find no immediate clues to my feeling. Apparently, my father, a foot away, eating popcorn at a measured pace, hadn't seen what I had. So I sat still, staring at the trailers, stunned, burning, isolated by the already vanished image, much like the saints were (as I understood it at the time) by visions, which Father Cassidy, our priest, made analogous to Ohio State games every Sunday, my head propped in my hands in the third row next to my father. It was the feeling I'd get entering beneath the soaring vault—to cooler, blue-and-gold-hued air, heavy with frankincense and smoke and a hazy but growing expectation that was somehow magnified by the chambered hush of the room, and the spectral shifting of cotton on lacquered wood, and the royal tones of the stained glass windows—but long dissolved by an overwhelming boredom.

I did not think any more of the woman that night, making it the last night for a long time that I was to be un-haunted by her image. Because for months afterward, I would be sitting at the kitchen island, squint-eyed, showered, dressed in my Catholic school uniform, ready to eat cereal made somehow nauseating by the chill of the tiles under my socked feet and the urchin-colored darkness outside; or at my desk, history, narrated in brief by Mr. Valentine, unfolding at the front of the room; or, most often, lying in bed before going to sleep, when the image of the woman would return. Somewhat. Her immersion in memory had morphed and softened her features enough that I doubted what I'd seen, and sometimes whether I'd seen it at all. In any case, with each momentary and repeated attempt to recall it, the image—like a face in a Dalí landscape, shifting and warping and receding the harder I concentrated on it—affected me more and more weakly. And so, there were nights that, with the same guilt and relief and satisfaction I would feel years later, when having woken in the early hours of the morning with a certain phrase ringing in my mind, I'd decide, as I went back to bed, that it was not worth the trouble of writing down, I would conclude I'd only imagined seeing on Channel 4 what I couldn't remember clearly in any case.

At that time, my mother entered into a period in which she rarely left her room. So my father had started dropping me off at school on his way to work, thirty minutes earlier than I was used to. And instead of waiting for my mother to pick me up, I had started taking the school bus back in the afternoons. It was on one such afternoon, riding the bus home—my head against the vibrating metal armature of the next bench, a hot rhombus of sunlight rumpling in my lap—that the woman returned to me in totality, or rather, since the image had been deformed beyond recognition, a nearly perfect echo of the image. As the robe dropped, I felt my breathlessness and diffidence as before something awful I'd done, some great crime I'd committed.

Stunned into a fugue, I walked down the block from the bus stop, careful to neither examine the feeling too closely and dissolve it under scrutiny, nor look at anything in the neighborhood long enough to be carried off into my habitual sense of existence. My eyes stayed unfocused as I turned (pretending not to see the timid wave of the elderly widower, Peter, who was often outside trimming bushes already Brunelleschian in the absolute symmetry of their lines, or raking a yard barren of leaves, and who with painful self-effacement would sometimes invite me to look at albums of himself and his deceased, Edna, standing in the sepia-toned light of the 1970s, in Rome, in Bucharest) into the former carriageway that led to our garage, our neighborhood passing far outside of me like a gallery of the mediocre Impressionism—featuring railroad crossings intersected by shadows, or the storefronts of the older buildings on Clifton Boulevard in peacock hues—that the *artistes* of our suburb of Cleveland worked in and which my mother had, at one point in her life, before the onset of these frequent episodes of being tired, patronized with gentle condescension, being herself an artist, but of glass.

That day, as I walked up the pathway to the door, I feared my mother would be feeling better, for the sight of her, at the stove, looking back at me from the pot of pasta sauce she was stirring, radiating normality, would, I sensed, inevitably destroy the delicate feelings I'd managed to transport safely from the bus stop. But when I entered the house and saw the unused stove in the unlit kitchen, I knew my mother was still upstairs and had to stifle my violent elation in order to preserve what impelled me to the living room for so vague a purpose that, after turning on the TV, muting it, and changing it to Channel 4, the static wasn't on for more than a minute before I lost completely the sense of what I had been pursuing so that I couldn't recall if I had even been looking for anything real in the first place. I was watching cartoons by the time my father's arrival made me look up.

"Did you do your homework?"

Sprawled out on the tartan chair, I shook my head.

He sat down. "Where's your mother?" he said. But he seemed to have asked the question out of the same indifferent politeness that causes people to ask how each other's days are going. And indeed, without seeming to acknowledge my reply, he turned the television to Channel 5, which transitioned to local news before the game shows began. The sunlight, by then having passed over the roofs of the houses across the street, and under the lip of our porch, narrowed to a band on the floor that I stared at in the descending gloom, feeling myself, without knowing why, on the verge of weeping, my sense of hopelessness only doubled by the wordless knowledge that I wanted to punish my father with this crying, and that therefore I would be inconsolable, for I wouldn't allow him to console me.

But just as the light on the floor narrowed to a thread, and I could feel—with a thrill—tears welling up, a creak ran through the ceiling. My father and I looked up. The water ran for a time in my parent's bathroom then shut off. Eventually, a toilet flushed. Footsteps approaching the staircase made my father stand. And forgetting my mysterious and already forgotten desire to punish him, I stood, too, elated, turning to him for the pleasure of seeing my elation reflected in his face. But he did not acknowledge my look, watching, as he was, the bizarre movements of something on the stairs. As the jerky approximations of a marionette's walk both parrot and parody the movements of a real body, so that there is something both humorous and tragic about their clumsiness that somehow implicates the larger figures watching them, so the movements of my mother on our staircase divided the seemingly uncomplicated action of stepping down stairs into painful false starts and uncanny retractions so that watching it I could not understand for a moment how anybody could move naturally down stairs at all.

My mother, her head bowed as she placed her foot down on the next stair, looked up. My father sat down. I joined him. *Seinfeld* was on. My father loved *Seinfeld*. Though he must have seen that particular episode ten or so times, he began to laugh at Kramer's entrance as my mother staggered down the stairs and through the periphery of our vision into the kitchen where she was going to make us dinner.

88   My father, who had very few friends, had attained a professional respect that wholly excluded people's opinions of his personality, and perhaps even relied, as a dramatic background against which his competence shone, on a general antipathy that he did not know he was cultivating. And so it ended up that year as in other years that he was to represent the university at a business conference, this time in New Delhi, where he would stay at the Grand New Delhi, and from which he was to return with the story about the reading light that would further cement the general antipathy toward him that had worked, without his knowledge, so well to his advantage.

It was during one night the week he was gone that, sitting on the toilet after having woken up, a resonantly falsetto stream of urine ringing below, the robe dropped once more in my memory. I looked around the dark bathroom, bewildered, my palms filled with sweat, as if I'd woken a second time, and now in a way that made going back to bed impossible. After sitting on the toilet for a time, waiting for the feeling to pass, the notion of what I might find on the television at that moment gradually occupying the entirety of my thoughts, I left the bathroom and slipped past my parents' room, which my mother had retreated to earlier that day just after making me dinner, and which she was unlikely to emerge from until late the next day.

With the sinking feeling that usually accompanies the realization of what we had until then only fantasized about, I turned on the TV, muted it, and typed in the 0 then the 4, already visualizing the static that would represent the divergence of my life from my fantasies. But it was as if, somewhere between the bathroom and the living room, I had fallen back into dreaming, where every desire and question and fear is somehow given an answer—though rarely the ones we expect. The static obediently and at once jumped to the image of a woman, different this time, whose chest was gradually filling the screen, where her hands were working absently at her buttons, for a purpose I could not guess. But I sensed whatever this purpose was would answer the feeling that what was about to happen was meant uniquely for me and would indeed guide the course of my life. I groaned when the image skipped and dissolved, fearing, for the first of many times, that this desire of mine was as unfulfillable as it was unnamable. But, flirting, skipping, stabilizing, the image returned and the woman's shirt opened noiselessly, like no material on earth.

I heard then a berserk sound so wrenchingly incongruous with what I was seeing that I thought I was hearing the collapse of my heart. But the shrieking went on and I, too, continued to live. I scrambled to pick up the remote to mute what I realized, as I was about to hit the button, wasn't a freak of static from the television, nor my heart, nor a passing brigade of fire trucks, but a person. My mother, upstairs, was shrieking, "CUT MY LEGS OFF. JUST CUT THEM OFF OR FUCKING KILL ME, BASH MY FUCKING HEAD IN I WANT IT TO STOP."

When it ended, I stood in the dying afterglow of the television screen I had turned off, at some point, without noticing. A silence settled over the house. I could hear a car passing down one of the side streets, where at night the intersections blinked yellow. As I waited, I became more and more unsure of whether I'd actually heard what I'd heard, for despite thinking that I'd recognized my mother's voice, the thought was arising, against my will, that perhaps I'd heard someone else, and my mother was not really in the house, and that perhaps, behind her closed door, something else was.

A creak ran through the ceiling, the sound drawing me, with a thrill, up the staircase as if by the strings of a puppet. I knew that if I returned to my room, went to bed, and woke up the next morning, life would go on as before. For I felt as if, downstairs, I had briefly and without knowing it wandered into someone else's life, and now,

90   as I gained the threshold to my room, then pulled the loose doorknob (which always left the smell of pennies on my hands) against its iron escutcheon so it would not rattle as I pushed it closed, I felt I was again gaining possession over my own. I paused, reassuring myself that my mother's door was still closed, as it always was on the occasions of her tiredness; the only other occasion I'd found it closed being on a night, years before these episodes of my mother's started, when I got terribly and mysteriously ill after waking from a nightmare about a butterfly that landed on a branch before me (I was invisible; I existed only as a perspective), the butterfly not growing larger, but the lens of the dream growing tighter and tighter around the butterfly until it occupied the totality of my attention, blotting out the slate blue sky behind it, the slow opening and closing of its wings as dizzying as the lowering and raising of drawbridges. When I could finally move out of the paralysis of my terror, I walked down the hall and found, as if only to continue my sense of unreality, the door to my parents' room closed. I realized I had been hearing low murmuring sounds from within after I knocked but then there was a sudden silence. My mother opened the door wearing a long shirt.

When she asked what was wrong, I could barely answer her. The alien tone of annoyance in her voice only worsened my sense of having woken to a further dream, possibly more disturbing because it was the obverse of my waking life in which my mother kindly acquiesced to the slightest whim I had. But with the hope of disproving this feeling, I described my dream, by the end of which my mother, with an unfamiliar blandness, told me I was fine and to go back to bed.

Instead of leading me back to my room, where she would have imbued my bed, which I now found hateful and full of disquiet, with the sense of impregnable security and comfort she normally radiated, she shut the door on me. And indeed, not long after I lay down, I started to feel

ill, this illness only worsened by the thought that my mother wouldn't
want to console me when I inevitably sought her comfort again, so I
was left with a false choice between lying alone in unbearable unease
and disturbing her and risking her anger, which I felt radiating even
from the stillness of the door when I knocked to explain I wasn't feeling
well, this illness getting worse each time my mother told me—my father
breathing from somewhere behind her in the dark, on the bed—that I
was fine and sent me back to my room where I could feel the sickness
spreading like oil over the cool salubrious feeling that my sheets had
once, in a former era, given me.

"Christopher?"

Still standing in my doorway, the door not yet closed, I waited,
afraid I had missed her next words in the thunder of my heart, so loud
was its beating. Afraid, too, she had said something that indicated she
knew without a doubt I was awake and therefore I was only causing
myself to be punished and increasing my punishment with my silence.

"Christopher, are you there?"

While I knew she knew I was awake and could hear her, I also
knew, by the uncertainty in her voice, that if I remained silent, she
wouldn't open the door, and if she didn't open the door so that I knew
she knew I was awake, and that she knew I knew that I'd heard her, the
next morning it would be as if I really hadn't heard her, as if she really
hadn't called out to me, as if I hadn't simply waited for the moment to
pass, which it would in a silence that, if it did not entirely obliterate
her words and my failure to answer them, would at least obscure them
from both of us in the same way the click of the latch bolt sliding home
into the faceplate of my door would be, in the morning, just one more
of those night sounds that in daylight lose all existence.

"Answer me—please?"

Years later, visiting my father in Baltimore, where he had retired from a subsequent job at a different university, I asked him what he remembered of living in that house. It was the last morning of my stay, and the weak light of February was filling his kitchen where he had made me coffee before I was to take the train home. He had asked, earlier, how often I spoke to my mother, and how she was doing, the conversation gradually making its way back toward Cleveland, where we had lived for so long together when I was a child. "The brass light-switch plates," he said, with a wistful smile I didn't share, for, until then, I had entirely forgotten about the light-switch plates as I had so many other things from that time, which—with those words of his, like those of an enchantment—returned to me from their oblivion. It always gave him, my father was saying, a curiously childlike and peaceful feeling to reach out to the light switch in the middle of some ordinary day, and—as if he had wandered into a fairy tale—find himself in miniature, trapped in the silent panel of brass, reaching back out to himself. ❧

....

Michael Sears lives in Los Altos, California. "Channel 4" is his first fiction in print.

OBJECT PERMANENCE

LUIZA FLYNN-GOODLETT

Yes, the red-tail who swooped across
our windshield didn't *actually* vanish
in the gulley, circles still. And when

the alarm wakes you, I trust that soft
nest of curls will be safely conveyed
to hover at a chalkboard, fall in your

eyes. But the calls keep getting closer.
So straighten your tie, hope we aren't
followed again and someone hears our

voices before seeing you in the ladies'
room. Maybe this is what mom meant
by, *I don't want your life to be harder.*

Driving, you didn't see that the hawk
veered just in time, so wear it lightly—
an asterisk's pronged, golden crown.

···
Luiza Flynn-Goodlett is editor-in-chief of Foglifter Press, and lives in Oakland. Her most recent chapbook is Twice Shy *(Nomadic Press).*

PEOPLE IN PROCESS

NATHAN HELLER

From the late 19th century until the middle of the 20th, the part of San Francisco now called South of Market was the center of the city's productive life. Unlike the elegant Victorian homes on residential hills, structures here were functional, solid, boxy. The neighborhood absorbed trade from the nearby wharves and produced iron and machine parts. After an earthquake in 1906, the community rebuilt itself in the image of industrial dynamism, temporary workers finding homes among more rooted families. The place got its continuity from transience; its eclecticism gave it shape. The Gold Rush hordes that had settled the area, mostly in tents, called it Happy Valley. The name was lost, but, over the years, the sentiment remained.

By the time Janet Delaney, a photographer, arrived in San Francisco in the late 1960s, South of Market was taken up in changes of a less dynamic kind. Working-class jobs that had held the neighborhood together had begun to disappear. Windows in warehouses shuttered and then shattered; streets once busy with commuters emptied out. A new kind of community emerged, and in the 1980s she captured its growth in a series of remarkable photographs, taken as she roamed the neighborhood with her camera. Delaney was living in the South of Market district then, along with other artists. In that sense, she herself became part of a new wave of productive culture taking root.

Her photographs, many of which appeared in her book *South of* **95**
Market (MACK Books, 2013), tell the stories of a landscape whose
fragile harmony didn't fit postcard ideals of beauty. In those original
photographs (printed here on the upper leaf of each pairing), we see
the district's old industrial landscape crumbling—sometimes literally,
sometimes through absence: an emptiness on streets that once would
have been busy, a haunting vacancy on counter stools or benches. Still,
as her lens found, productive life went on. We encounter these images
today and are reminded, first, how different the *scale* of urban living
was before every inch of space sold at a premium. Middle-class people
exist here with room around them; there's a casual openness and an
airiness to the indoor scenes that is instantly recognizable as being of
an era different from our own.

The lower leaf of each pair is a photograph that Delaney took more
recently, giving some sense of the South of Market district—SoMa, in its
current portmanteau—in the thrall of its more recent change. Starting
in the '90s, the neighborhood began to be home to a different style of
industry. Old warehouses were bought and repartitioned into offices.
New businesses serving new lifestyles appeared. Delaney left South of
Market, and San Francisco, when she could not afford it anymore. (Today
she lives in Berkeley.) In the photographs of 21st century SoMa, we see
fresh kinds of work being done in the old spaces. Emptiness remains,
but it is costly. Diversity remains, too, in the ethnic and origin sense,
although the range of habits and professions that it crosses appears to
have narrowed. In these images, captured by one person's eye—or, anyway,
one person, since creative vision itself changes over time—we find a
record of a neighborhood adjusting to the demands of our current age.

For all the difference, though, what's startling is how much is the
same. A ghostly fog still looms out the windows. The landscape is still
always being remade. South of Market looks nothing like it did when

96   it was Happy Valley, filled with wishful, transient people. But in other ways—maybe even in the ways that matter most—the neighborhood has stayed true to its founding restlessness, its unsettled ideals. ✂

JANET DELANEY

THEN AND NOW

<hr>

Flag Makers, Natoma at 3rd Street, 1982
wow, Natoma Alley at 3rd Street, 2013

·

Helen and her husband, Chester, at the Helen Café, 486 6th Street, 1980
Young Woman at Lunch Counter, New Montgomery Street, 2013

·

Bobbie Washington and her daughter Ayana, 28 Langton Street, 1982
Interior, One Hawthorne Luxury Condos, 645 Howard Street, 2013

·

Longtime neighbors, Langton at Folsom Street, 1981
Waiting for the Art Academy Bus, New Montgomery Street, 2016

·

Shantiben Dahyabhai Patel, Park Hotel, 1040 Folsom Street, 1980
211 Main Street, 2014

·

Color Trend, 2nd at Harrison Street, 1986
In Conversation, ThoughtWorks, 814 Mission Street, 2016

·

Saturday afternoon, Howard between 3rd and 4th Streets, 1981
Convention on Howard, between 3rd and 4th Streets, 2016

·

Mercantile Building, Mission and 3rd Streets, 1980
Mercantile Building under Renovation, from Yerba Buena Park, 2017

<hr>

Nathan Heller is a New Yorker staff writer and contributing editor to Vogue. He is at work on a book about the Bay Area for Penguin Press.

THIS IS WHY WE CAN'T HAVE NASTY THINGS

CHARLIE JANE ANDERS

66 **I** have something to tell you. I'm leaving. I still love you. But I can't love this city anymore." She gestures around, indicating the remains of San Francisco.

Smoke break. Wanda and I pass a pre-roll back and forth on the sidewalk in a crowd of five people: girls in skimpy club wear, guys in either track pants or crinkled business suits that they clearly just wore on an airplane. A homeless guy watches us from across the street, the same dude who was just telling us the city seized all his belongings, after we gave him twenty bucks.

"I can't help loving this town," I say. "I'm one of those weird people who's a slut except when it comes to cities."

"Yeah, but." Wanda blows a hot, fragrant, invisible cloud. "They killed our bar."

Glamrock isn't actually dead yet, but it's holding its own wake tonight. This sticky-floored, railroad-car-shaped dive bar has nurtured and protected (and sometimes annoyed) generations of trans girls, punk sluts, sex workers, drag performers, strippers, and random queers. It's the sort of place where the bathroom stalls have no doors, so nobody can have sex or do drugs inside them. And it's going out of business next week. San Francisco used to have a million pockets and folds in her long flowery skirts, where the strange and barely loved could create their own reality. But lately, not so much.

"This is why we can't have nasty things," Wanda grumbles. The joint burns all the way down to her fingertips, so she tosses it and heads back inside, and I follow.

Random memories overwhelm me when I venture inside Glamrock. Over here, on this tiny stage, I did my first and last performance in the Friday night drag show (which was mostly trans women), lip-synching to an old Sheena Easton song about walls made of sugar. Over there, some creepy dude grabbed my ass, under my tiny pleather skirt and thong, and demanded to know about the status of my genitalia. The back corner, with the long bench against the mirrored wall, where I used to hide with five or six trans friends from the Brat Army, snarking about everything.

And right here, by the women's room with the busted hand-dryer, is where I met Wanda for the first time ever. They were playing an old Destiny's Child song and something shifted inside me when I saw her long dark hair, huge false lashes, and fuck-everything smile. I can't describe the feeling in terms of a physical sensation, except that it was like there was this valve inside me that had rusted shut, maybe never opening fully since the end of adolescence, and suddenly someone grabbed a pair of pliers and yanked it all the way to the left. Something flowed that was warmer than blood and twice as oxygenated. My head floated. I felt Destiny's Child in the soles of my feet.

We danced on and off surfaces, with and without rhythm, eyes open and eyes closed, until our hands became petals for our stamen faces.

I couldn't believe Wanda actually wanted to go home with me, out of all the pervert stars in this place. Mouths glued together, hands on each other's elbows, grunting and giggling as we rolled around my futon.

But we also never left this bar at all, or at least we always came back here, every weekend and many weeknights. Dating Wanda meant getting to know every filthy inch of this place, and the names and backstories of a few dozen semi-regulars. Our whole relationship centered on this one watering hole.

There are places where you go to get picked up, or to pick someone up—but then, if you spend enough time in them, you find yourself getting adopted instead. Becoming part of a whole scene.

I told this to Wanda, and she laughed. "Sometimes the best communities come out of people just trying to get laid. I love that moment where we start taking care of each other instead of only wanting to fuck each other." Wanda works as a graphic designer, and her phone is full of work contacts—but also, people she had sex with five years ago, who will still drop everything to help her move a refrigerator. "That's how it works."

It's true. Back when I met Wanda, I had so many lovers that I had no more bandwidth for all their problems, like Gravy was getting evicted and Jeri's bedframe shattered and Roxie was getting evicted and Susie's water heater broke down and ZQ was getting evicted and Frankie's truck was making a noise like one of those truffle-sniffing pigs all the time, and also Frankie was getting evicted, too. I couldn't be there for all of them. So I started just networking them with each other, like I got Frankie to replace the bedframe while Gravy fixed Frankie's truck, and I was also sleeping with a housing rights attorney named Trini who helped everyone fight their evictions. I basically became a referral service among the people I was fucking.

Inside Glamrock, everybody mourns, raising dirty shot glasses to catch the flickering black light and dancing on their stools to the club music. Rikki hugs two people at a time, Wilmot keeps buying me drinks, Jezz wants to take selfies in front of the neon sign with anyone who comes near. "I'm seriously going to have no place to go anymore where I don't feel like an endangered species," Angela yells over the vintage techno.

We drink and drink, but we don't get drunk, because Glamrock has always watered its drinks like tropical ferns.

The next smoke break, Wanda starts talking about all her lovers who live in other cities: the cute enby in Portland, the soft-bearded boi in Detroit, and so on. Maybe it's time to become poly-itinerant, or poly-nomadic. Poly-peripatetic? Traveling around from lover to lover, living nowhere except for a dozen sweeties' bedrooms, all over the place. Wanda has a job that she can do anywhere and an apartment she doesn't mind abandoning, unlike me. Every city a different body.

"You're really just going to up and leave?" I say. The neon sign sputters and goes off for a moment.

"I'll come back." Wanda looks into the gutter. "You can be one of the lovers I visit."

I don't want to be a way station. I don't want to have to reconnect and disconnect, over and over. I want to be the place where Wanda comes to rest.

As long as we never leave this bar, it'll never be over. I order another round of drinks and start singing along with Whitney Houston, trying to draw Wanda deeper into the gloomy back area. Every well-worn dance song that comes on the crackly speakers is my favorite, every tiny occurrence is another excuse for a toast. I point out the spot where Wilmot bonked his head on Trizzie's stiletto heels, and the burn mark on the carpet from the Great Violet Wand Disaster of 2017. The warm darkness closes in around us, the arch corned-beef scent could almost be all the nourishment we might ever require.

It's settled. We'll just stay here forever, at the Glamrock.

"We should get going," Wanda says in my ear. "Almost closing time."

The last-call bell clangs, loud enough to echo off the heavy ceiling beams.

"We can't go yet!" I tug at her sleeve. "One more dance, one more drink, I think I figured out how we can give each other mutual lap dances at the same time. Come on, the night is—"

But Wanda is already hustling me out the front door, toward the future. I wish I could take her someplace else that would change her mind, some art event that lasts twenty-four hours and turns your eyes to stained glass if you stay the whole time. Some beer bust where the Sisters pull a brand-new hanky code out of the center of the roast goat carcass and the first person to decode it gets to assign everyone else a new kink. I wish there was an Anon Salon happening now, or an underground dungeon party, or a body-painted literary festival.

"I remember when cities used to be prisms, or warrens," Wanda says. "I don't even know what a city is supposed to be now. Maybe every city is better visited than lived in these days."

Nobody will write a huge tribute to Glamrock, or put up a plaque. This neighborhood will barely notice it's gone. Some other, fancier bar will occupy that space, and be objectively better in almost every way, except for drink prices and clientele.

I can't begin to quantify what I'm about to lose. Angela and Jezz file out of the bar, heads bowed and arms folded against the night wind. I don't know when I'll see either of them again, or where I'll be hanging out after next week. Wanda is the one, of the two of us, who would put in the work to identify our new dive bar, someplace to transplant as much of our scene as possible.

The anticipation of loneliness, surrounded by the people who will soon be gone, is maybe worse than actual loneliness. You can't get used to something that hasn't even started yet.

Begging Wanda to stay will do no good, which only makes me more anxious to beg. *We can make our own San Francisco*, I want to say. *We can become the thing this city can't get rid of.*

I'm still trying to think of a way to petition Wanda when she gets there first. "Promise me something," she says.

"Umm ... okay."

"Promise me you'll go out, a lot. Wear that skirt you used to wear when I first knew you. Lip-synch to 'Sugar Walls' again, or some other terrible eighties song about sex. Keep in touch with all these people. Make a terrible scene that people need a whole hashtag to complain about. When I come back in a few months, I want you to give me a tour of all the sites of your disgrace. Okay?"

"Okay." She holds out her hands and I take them, and we both lean forward until we're kissing. The wind picks up, and the air runs colder, and Wanda and I huddle together. She smells of booze and weed and rose petals, and for a moment we're both completely at rest, wrapped in each other. The neighborhood is quieting down, except for a late-night hipster meatball place and a group of young straight people who just got kicked out of their own bar. We can't stay out here.

"Let me take you home," I mumble, and Wanda nods, and we find a taxi. The driver is playing the same '90s dance music as the DJ at Glamrock, and Wanda starts to dance inside the constraint of her seatbelt. ✄

....

Charlie Jane Anders is the author of All the Birds in the Sky *(Tor Books) and, most recently,* The City in the Middle of the Night *(Tor Books), and lives in San Francisco.*

TRAUMA NOTE

SARA MUMOLO

I can't write the way my sister can do kundalini yoga.

I can't do yoga the way I can smoke.

I love to smoke.

There's a smoking section in heaven, I swear,

The way I feel nothing.

Can't you see what I'm getting at?

I'm still here, autocorrecting.

The way bed corrects to her.

Yes, I can't keep anything confidential. It's so tempting to tell me, a voice other than your own to shout out all your secrets. Check out my moves.

The lion takes a shower.

The lion screams and cries. These are all sight words.

Let it all in. It's already pouring in here.

I know. I started the poem again.

It's just that we all know how good it feels to degrade oneself for the reader. Speaker. Strange.

Pass me the bread and wine already. I'm craving bodies and blood. Is this the poem where you show up empty-handed?

When I hit the pigeon with my SUV its feathers cascade across the windshield, over the tents near Starline Social Club,

and I don't think about the repercussions of what I am saying, where I am saying it. The socialites, the gas guzzler, the homeless building homes out of whatever they can. People just want to be together, okay?

I can't believe I wasn't there when you put your hands on the asphalt and tried to sit up. I wasn't there as you lifted your torso from the pavement. Someone found you. Someone was there with you, I think. Skateboard pieces catty corner, slivered.

The priest tells us that god takes the young to spare them from horrendous future sins. Can you believe that shit? I was there for that.

My aunt makes sure I have new shoes for the service. She buys me Doc Martens. I just remembered that. Her closet packed full of photo albums full of dead people who all look like people sleeping, people with closed eyes laying on white pillows, hair, limbs, languid across sheets.

In the dream I can't speak the way I can while awake. In the dream you are shirtless and speaking, but I can't hear you. My aunt says you're really there. Sometimes your friend sleeps next to me, and I think this is the wrong world. I can fuck this up for you, too, grief tells me.

Sara Mumolo is the author of the poetry collection Day Counter *(Omnidawn) and is the associate director for the MFA Creative Writing Program at St. Mary's College of California.*

POSTHUMOUS

GLORIA FRYM

When a great writer dies and was a close friend, a confidant, even one's mentor, the posthumous reviews and articles about their work and life leave one bewildered.

No, they leave one bereft of commentary.

Even writing the preceding sentence I couldn't use the first person. I couldn't initially write that this leaves *me* confused. Why? Why can't I feel the joy others feel about the selected works, so carefully assembled, having garnered two reviews and a separate article in *The New York Times* and ten other outstanding reviews in important venues during the last days *before* the official publication date? Why do I feel nausea, even sadness masked as neutrality, with each new notice of the book?

She wanted her stories to have a wider audience. And she wanted more critical notice. What writer doesn't? Though she loved to gossip, what she abhorred most was gossip about her person, which eventually returned to her through our mutual circle of friends and acquaintances. She was quick to figure out who said what about her, who embellished, though often couldn't remember who she told what. She left strict instructions in her will that no one be allowed to write a biography of her, especially X, who was famous for swooping down on dying writers, especially friends, and beating others to the punch with his bios. Most every recent review points out that the work is remarkable, sensational;

114 how come we haven't heard of her before, read her before, read her if you only read one book this summer. And that the work is autobiographically based, as if most writers don't prey on their own experience for material.

None of this bothers me, specifically. That there's a social media page devoted to her, that new photos of her pop up daily accompanying the reviews, even ironically contradicting the reviews—a gorgeous, sweet-looking young woman holding her diapered baby—the image belies the grit, mordant humor, and emotional violence of her writing.

That she didn't have many female friends doesn't bother me now. She was of a generation and mind that didn't quite trust women, especially women writers. She felt betrayed by several, for one reason or another, such as that famous poet who lived upstairs and told her she'd never be happy. She didn't trust men, either, except for male writers who adored her raw-edged writing, her public feminine demeanor—always accommodating mixed with profound wit—and she could weave a story like one of the guys, drink hard like one of the guys. She had lived hard, as they say, sometimes off the grid. She never had daughters, only sons who adored her.

No, that doesn't bother me. It did when she was alive.

If I say to others, to students, write to find out, write what you can't know otherwise, write into the unknown—forget the clichés of "finding your voice" and "write what you know"—I should take my own advice here and untangle my feelings. As a young writer, I couldn't even turn interviews into prose—I was repulsed at telling the same "material" again. If I'm holding my feelings in suspense by the progression of this narrative, it's that I'm hoping some phrase or sentence, even a single word, will give me what I want. Will help me relay my discomfort during this moment of acclaim the work of my late friend is enjoying. "Dying," says writer friend Andrei Codrescu about a prolific poet who crashed his car into a tree at twenty-four, somewhat James Dean-like, "is a drastic way of getting your works into print."

Which brings up The Death Effect. "Is dying really a shrewd career move?" wrote Terry Teachout. I don't believe so. But then that's just me. Wasn't it John Kennedy O'Toole who won a 1981 posthumous Pulitzer long after he committed suicide in 1969? His mother struggled to get his works into print. Baudelaire, Rimbaud, Van Gogh, Kafka, Marx, Jim Thompson, Poe, Dickinson—an endless list of artists whose work achieved fame only after they died.

We do like our writers better if they're dead.

The success of my friend's work, says another writer friend, Summer Brenner, can be summed up thusly: it's a fairy tale without a princess.

I wish I didn't know how much anguish each story the Princess wrote cost her and others. I wish I had no idea of how cruelly one of her husbands treated her and what a nasty man he was and how she took care of him, decades after they divorced, until he died. And in his will he left her nothing. He was a perfect replica of her mother—a mean-to-the-core alcoholic, crippled by her small-mindedness and racism, selfish. She instructed her attendant to have her cremated before her daughters could arrive to make a funeral.

Sometimes knowing too much belies the notion that The Truth Shall Make You Free. I'm bound, entrapped, imprisoned in what I know and what I witnessed and how I saw it then, and how I see it now.

I often speak to her, because so much happens that she'd love to know. It's easy to tell her about the new Portuguese writer—well, new to me—I've been reading, and might have probably been new to her, but maybe not, because she'd read everything. Once I visited her grave. It was deeply emotional because she is buried next to a great poet, her own mentor and advocate. We're family, in some way. And I want to say to her, you were so right about many things that I sometimes dismissed as old-fashioned. She was a generation older, didn't believe in "quality time" with your kids, didn't believe in entertaining them, always wrote thank-you notes by hand, loved moving and redecorating, hated orangey-yellow flowers, loved fuchsia and high heels and bright pink lipstick and expensive perfume, Coco by Chanel, eyebrow pencil, settees, pancake make-up, Elmore Leonard and Anthony Trollope.

Whenever I touch Velcro, I think of a desperate moment in her life when she needed a job. She imagined she could teach again in the public schools after a hiatus of decades. Though her existence was no fairy tale then, she was sober for many years. She did well, she said, on the state test. For the essay part, she chose the question, What was the most important invention of the 20th century? She wrote about Velcro from every angle she could think of in the allotted time. She was sure she aced it. When the test results arrived, the examiners had failed her. They thought she didn't take the topic seriously, that she was mocking the test, and therefore the profession. A person who did that with a history like hers (she was honest on her application) would not be somebody to whom our children should be entrusted.

Everyone who knew her has their stories. I have so many I ache. They bring her alive in ways I couldn't anticipate. Hearing her read one of her stories on tape reconstituted her entirely—one forgets the actual voice of the gone, perhaps remembering a gesture, a laugh more clearly. Or a couple of syllables, indelible in the mind's ear, a morning hull-o. The color of the eyes brought out even brighter by a piece of matching jewelry or shirt. From behind, the last time one saw her walking away, unsteady. A recent photo dug up by the estate featured her in the act of writing. She was left-handed! Why had I never noticed? Had I never seen her actually write? She always wrote first by hand, had no patience for machinery, claimed to have lost volumes on the computer. It all went away. As she did.

And now in this new fairy tale existence, the publisher has put out buttons you can wear saying Read X; Amazon has run out of the book in less than two days; a British publisher has made a cover in the style of clothing labels.

Foreign rights were sold, soon to be translated into ten languages. Each new development irritates me. Why? It's not jealousy. I am a writer who loves when writers and artists I know win big awards, when they sell books to major publishing houses, get great advances, great reviews. It's what Hinduism calls Darshan. I like the success of my friends; it might rub off on me. Only this one is different. This friend can't enjoy the major splash her work has made. In one minute, a movie script will be written and optioned. In another, someone will gather her letters and publish them.

Though she taught for a time, when she thought a story didn't work, she just said, It doesn't work, I don't know why. ("I don't believe it," as Jack Spicer liked to say.) Only if she thought a piece was good would she offer suggestions—mainly edits—to make it better. She simply didn't have the energy to be a detailed editor. When she was too depressed or in pain from her numerous and serious health problems to give much, she either "adored" a piece or "hated" it. But what she gave was akin to a blessing from the Dalai Lama. That's how I felt about her writing and her person. I loved her deeply. There was plenty of competition by other writers for her love.

During the dry spells, and who knows what causes them, what caused hers, she would use our acronym, IWNWA. How are you? I'd ask at the start of a phone conversation. Oh, she'd say, miserable, IWNWA. I WILL NEVER WRITE AGAIN.

Neither of us believed it. And now it's true.

The publisher of her selected stories took out an ad in *The New Yorker*. "An important American writer," it quotes above the salmon-colored replica of the book. Now it's a few weeks before Christmas. Her book has made the Top 100 on *The New York Times*, and their Ten

118 Most Notable as well, along with Ta-Nehisi Coates's *Between the World and Me*, and the fourth installment of a quartet she would have loved, *The Story of the Lost Child* by Elena Ferrante. A rare year for readers.

"But wider recognition eluded her," said one review, "during her life." Who's catching up with whom? We, her friends and the circle of small press people who knew her work, recognized her brilliance widely.

As for the reviews and articles, no one is getting it wrong, no, that's not it. It's not that reviewers have impugned her work somehow with any inept vision of it. To the contrary, all the reviews, especially the international press, have gotten it right, though most make too much of the proximity of the stories to her life and seem to concoct a biography of her, exhuming and extracting and confusing the person with the artist, which is always the trap of biography because the citizen and the artist are two separate entities. The "secrets" of impulse and construction are largely inviolable and mysterious—"the biographeed always flees the biographer," says Emily Dickinson.

It is something about writing and the dead and the living. One can easily prefer the work of dead authors. Writers themselves often look to reinvent the classics. But what do the deceased do to their writing? Perhaps we read the dead differently when we discover the details of their lives or deaths—the work takes on an aura it might never produce if the writer were alive. Perhaps knowing that Walter Benjamin committed a hasty suicide fleeing the Nazis or that Robert Walser spent most of his later years in a mental hospital gives the living work an extra melancholy we actually enjoy.

She would have been bemused by, even somewhat cynical about, all this, especially the buttons. Her gallows humor was tempered by her tone, often wistful, remote, yet utterly engaged. During the last clean but physically miserable years of her life, she was like Miles or Coleman doing "I'm a Fool to Love You" for ten minutes of understated ecstasy.

Lying on a grassy field next to her, among other writers on a Fourth of July, waiting for the high desert sun to fade and the fireworks to start, every explosion of color was *Dee-vine* and triggered another time in another city on another continent and a tale that might or might not be "true." But then, who cares? We only wanted her to tell it, because *the view from the balcony framed with lilac passion flower and crowded with red parrots in huge cages squawking Hola Hola Adios, looking out on the fuchsia bougainvillea twining up the Jacaranda in its last bloom, oh, and then the chauffeur, who I had a terrible crush on, he wore white gloves no matter the heat, buzzed at the front gate, and we were all—the children and maids—whisked off to the bullring for a grand spectaculo of fuegos artificiales which lasted for hours and hours, it was just Divine!*

Am I any closer to naming the feeling I began to investigate? Doubtful, but it is the whole of her, the literary and personal being I cherished. Who else would call you in the morning and regret the birthday present they'd given you the night before, a new translation of *Anna Karenina*? "I'm so sorry, I just finished it. Their translation is so dry. Forgive me!" Or the summer we decided to read *Moby Dick* together. Three days later, the phone rang early—she always got up by dawn. "Hi. I just finished it," she chirped. "No way," I said. "I'm barely in Chapter 8." "Way," she said. "What's the big deal?" She was a fast reader and read for a good part of the day, but this was impossible. "Listen," I said, "I have the Norton edition, which did you read?" After a small silence while she got the book off the shelf, she burst into laughter, and laughed hard and long, coughing and almost crying. She'd read an abridged version.

The whole of her is gone, but she has risen from the grave by acclaim, and I experience a kind of homesickness for her, a second and ironic loss of her. She no longer suffers the privation of existential incompleteness, of the transience of life. No. Her work is done, and she is immortal. ✄

....

Gloria Frym is a professor in the Writing & Literature Program at California College of the Arts. Her most recent book is The True Patriot *(Spuyten Duyvil). She lives in Berkeley.*

STRANGERS

NINA SCHUYLER

y son invited a strange boy to our house. Strange, in that the boy was only an acquaintance of Thomas's, not a good friend, and strange because Thomas had yet to invite his best friends to our new house. But he was coming, this boy who got locked out of his house and needed some place to stay until his mother got home.

It was 8 p.m., and the small brown bats were swooping between the fir trees, as if weaving an intricate net that had to be woven or the sky would fall and crush the world. Through the open window, I heard the howls of packs of coyotes hunting for rabbits. The other day, I'd woken to the high-pitched warble of the wild turkeys strutting the hills behind the house.

After the divorce, we—my fifteen-year-old son and I—moved from the middle of the small town of Fairfax to its edge. A rundown cottage, with old warped windows that held a hint of violet, and a slanted wood floor, as if the furniture would soon find itself bunched up on the right side of the house, it was full of personality with its quirks and odd nooks that would hold nothing more than three books. Living on the edge of civilization (that's what it felt like) was where I'd always wanted to be, and my main regret was that it had taken me forty-seven years to get here. That seemed true for all my women friends; a divorce or some significant upset birthed the life they'd longed for. Thomas, though, called it a dump. He said he would never invite anyone over.

I was in my study, a room of bookshelves and books, reading one of my student's stories, when I heard my son's voice in the garage, followed by a male voice, low and loud. I set the story aside and went out to meet this boy. Not a boy at all, he was slightly taller than Thomas, with thick, dark wavy hair, rosy cheeks, a handsome young man, with a broad chest, a broad mouth, a broad smile. He looked me in the eye—that counted a lot, a teenage boy who could look you in the eye, his eyes startling light topaz—and he extended his hand and said, "My name's Ben. Nice to meet you, Mrs. Sweeny."

"It's Ramsey now," I said. "I use my maiden name."

"Thank you for letting me come here."

Thomas looked stunned and shy, as if he didn't quite know what to do next.

"There's leftovers, if you're hungry," I said.

"I don't want to be any trouble," he said, glancing at Thomas.

Considerate, I thought. I liked him. "No trouble."

While Thomas and Ben watched a basketball game in the living room, I went to the kitchen to warm up leftovers. The house, with the excited chatter of the basketball commentators and Thomas and Ben talking about the game, was lively now, as if it had taken a long nap, and was now wide awake.

Ben ate the warmed-up roasted chicken. "This is so good."

Thomas shot me a look. I'd told Thomas I was finished making fancy meals, no more hours spent in the kitchen, coming up with new dishes, something I'd done for years.

"I'm glad you like it," I said coolly. But I was anything but cool; I was surprisingly pleased by his compliment and then thrown off by my reaction.

I went back to my study to work, but was half listening for Thomas and Ben. Soon, though, I was happily ensconced in a story about a woman who was recently widowed and had three small children. She lived on a farm and was so grief-stricken and bereft that she refused to think about her dead husband, a farmer who raised corn, refused to speak his name out loud, and eventually she forgot about him altogether. It was as if she'd never married, and when someone mentioned her husband's name, she looked at the speaker, baffled, as if the obliteration of her memory of him had been final. The story intrigued me, this idea of the complete erasure of a life. I supposed the attraction was its delicate fragrance of freedom.

When 10:00 came and went, I went out to the living room and offered to drive Ben home. His mother still wasn't home, he told me, his voice like a long, nervous laugh. "She's stuck at the office and hopes I can sleep here," he said. "If that's okay."

I'd never met his mother. Who was this woman who let her son stay at a stranger's house? How did she not fret about him—who he was with, what he was doing?

"Of course," I said. "Thomas, help me get a sleeping bag."

Thomas followed me down the hallway. "Are you okay with this?" I said.

"Sure, I mean, he's got nowhere else to go. Are you okay with this?" This last part dipped in sarcasm.

My son had begun to use gel in his hair, spiking it straight up, giving him another inch of height, so he towered over me. He spent hours in his room alone, and even when I confiscated his phone for the night, he remained in there, doing something—reading, I hoped, which he'd once enjoyed immensely, even willingly and happily talking about the books with me. But that was long ago. I'd come to view his bedroom as a womb, where he'd tucked himself away until the process of self-gestation was complete, and only then would he emerge, on his own terms. There were times I didn't particularly like the person who was emerging, but I had so little say in the matter. In some ways the process reminded me of a failing marriage, though unlike a marriage, there would be no divorce. My task was to give him a wide berth and remain an observer, passive, unless he dramatically overstepped.

I went back to my room, got ready for bed and soon fell asleep, only to be jarred awake by the floor boards creaking and moaning. I sat up, disoriented, the room so dark. The clock, 2:00 a.m. Ben was in my room, right beside my bed.

"What are you doing in here?"

At first, he didn't say anything, and I thought he might be sleepwalking.

"I can't sleep," he said. "Thomas snores."

That was true. I got up, grabbed my wrap, conscious of my thin, white nightgown, like gauze floating around me, and led him down the hallway to the living room, with a pillow and blankets tucked under my arm. In an instant, it seemed, he was asleep on the couch, stretched out on his side. He had long eyelashes, a beautiful symmetry to his face, and I imagined he had a girlfriend, and if not, many girls flittering and fluttering around him, trying to catch his eye. He let out a long exhale. The house was still, the refrigerator hummed. I felt my breathing slow, steady. Then I heard the coyotes howling—they were always moving, large packs at night, displaced from the never-ending construction. I imagined them sprinting on the dirt paths like veins on the hills, illuminated by the moon, sprinting to catch a rabbit, a mouse, sprinting for the sheer pleasure of sprinting.

In the morning, with both boys still sleeping, I got my coat and headed out. In the past, I would have made breakfast for my husband and son, done the dishes, the laundry—a good wife, until I couldn't anymore, because it felt like a pillow was pressed on my face, cutting off my oxygen. The sun was out, turning the world brilliant, and I didn't want to miss any of it. I stopped at Java Café and talked to one of the regulars who was reading a book about a woman who loved the characters in a book so much that reality began to fade for her. I wrote down the title. When I got back, the boys were gone. A note, "Gone to play basketball."

Throughout the day, the thought of Ben's mother tugged at me. It wasn't abandonment. After all, Ben was in high school, soon off to college. But it was something. Part of me envied her—how she could empty herself of her son, give herself over exclusively to herself again, like a young girl without a care in the world. Her attention, energy, time, mental space, she reclaimed it—it was all hers. She'd trusted the universe to provide, which, in fact, it did.

✿   ✿   ✿

I'd had a long day at work, teaching three classes, with finger-wringing students filing in my office, worrying about their stories. I loved their stories, loved puzzling over them with my students, but I was tired. Sun from the spring day hung low in the sky, as if it wanted one long look at the world before it disappeared. Thomas had basketball practice and wouldn't be home for another two hours. Solitude luxuriously stretched out in front of me, like an empty sugar-sand beach. I'd soak in a hot bath, let my mind become my own again. I'd write something. I'd been working on it in my mind, though it was inchoate.

I pulled in the driveway. Ben sat on the porch steps. He looked at me, an expression of expectation, hope, and embarrassment, the last emotion encapsulated by his gaze jumping from me to his white sneakers, a hole in the toe of the left one. I hesitated before opening the car door, feeling my plans for solitude deflate, dissolve. It was an ancient feeling, one that tainted my earliest memories.

"Thomas is at basketball," I said, getting out of the car.

He stood. "Okay." He didn't start walking away.

"Do you want a glass of water?" I said, giving in to my guilt.

"Sure. Thank you."

"Locked out again?" I said.

He nodded, but it was a slow nod, as if he wasn't sure about his answer. His white T-shirt was torn on his shoulder, revealing pale skin.

I offered Ben a peanut butter and jelly sandwich, Thomas's favorite when he was a boy. Ben wolfed it down, and I suspected it was his first meal of the day.

"Do you like him?" he said. I turned to see he was pointing at Raymond Carver's *Collected Short Stories* sitting on the counter.

I realized I'd made assumptions about Ben—not academically inclined, not a reader, maybe even prone to skipping school—and they were probably all wrong. "I love anyone who can transport me elsewhere," I said. I told him I taught creative writing at the university.

He looked at me intently, as if taking in this information and deciding something. I handed him the book.

"Oh, 'Viewfinder,'" he said. "The guy on the roof, throwing rocks. I love that one."

I sipped my wine. "Why?"

"Well, you know, after doing nothing, sitting in that empty house, everyone gone, his family gone, he finally does something. Even if it's just throwing rocks from the top of his roof. And it's the perfect action. Throwing rocks, all his rage and anger."

Ben said when his father left them, his mother threw all his clothes in the backyard. A mountain on the grass—suits, shirts, shoes, ties, sweaters. This happened when he was nine years old, and at the time, he was mad at his mother, but now, looking back, he was happy she'd done something. "You can't live your life with the wrong person."

126 His topaz eyes, three decades younger than mine, but wizened by experience.

He said his dad remarried and lived in Florida. "The same unhappy guy, though."

"Do you miss him?" After the divorce, Thomas's father had moved to Paris and enrolled in culinary school. Though they talked on the phone, Thomas hadn't seen him in over a year. I asked Thomas's father how he could stand it, not seeing his son, and he said he was too busy right now with his coursework. Like Ben's mother, I thought. The banishment of the son. Maybe it wasn't a matter of emptying oneself out, but filling oneself up with something else.

"No." He took a bite of his sandwich. "Are you divorced, too?"

"Yes."

"That's probably why Thomas and I get along so well. Same type of family."

I suspected Thomas held a different view of their relationship.

He took a drink of water. "Why did you divorce?"

I'd become used to our frank conversation and decided to answer honestly, as honestly as I could. I felt he deserved it. In fact, I preferred honesty to chatter. That was a pet peeve of my ex-husband's: my inability to make small talk. He'd said I'd known how to do it at the beginning of our marriage and had a lot more friends because of it. I told him what was latent and smoldering could manifest, especially over a stretch of sixteen years, moving from background to foreground.

"The answer to that question depends on the day," I said.

Ben smiled.

"What?" I said.

He said it confirmed what he'd always thought, but few people agreed with him. That the idea of the self was a fiction. A made-up thing. People were always changing, but it scared the shit out of them,

so they had to tell themselves there was a solid thing called the self. **127**
But it just wasn't true.

It felt as if I was talking to one of my colleagues at work, so I gave
Ben the most recent version of why we'd divorced: if marriage is a
story, I fell out of the story. It was hard to say why or how it happened,
but it happened.

"That's pretty vague," he said.

"It is, but that's how it feels today." On other days, I told myself
it was my husband who fell out of the narrative. I'd also suspected I
wasn't cut out for marriage: it was probably too much to ask of anyone
to admire, let alone love, my capacity for solitude.

"My dad cheated on my mom," he said.

He seemed happy with this answer, and it made me curious how
Thomas talked about my divorce.

"How's your mom doing?" I said.

"Good. Moving on. She's a therapist. She works a lot."

I'd always thought it would be awful to have parents who were
therapists; the private world always under siege. I asked him about
it, and Ben said it was fine. He mostly kept things to himself, and his
mother had plenty of patients to take care of, so it worked out.

"Your private world must come out in your writing," he said.

"Yes, but it's always disguised."

He smiled, as if I'd revealed something significant, intimate, and
slightly risqué.

When I said I had some work to do, he got up, took his plate to
the sink, and headed for the door. I had the urge to hug him goodbye.

Later, when Thomas came home, I told him Ben had stopped by.

"Weird."

"Why?"

"He knows I have basketball," he said. "He's not that good of a

128 friend, you know."

"Maybe he could be," I said.

Ben, with his unloved shirt, was an intelligent, thoughtful, reflective young man. I had a sense that whatever the topic—literature, politics, religion—he could hold his own.

"No," said Thomas, his tone adamant.

"Why not?"

He stared at me, as if deciding whether I could possibly possess the intelligence to understand what he had to say. "You really want me to be friends with someone like him?"

I felt something swell out behind Thomas's words, like a dark, ominous cloud.

"What's wrong with him?" I said, hearing my defensive tone.

"He latches onto whoever's nice to him. He's like a chameleon. I mean, whatever you want to do, he'll say he wants to do it, too. He plays basketball with me, just because I like it. When he's with this other guy at school who loves video games, that's all Ben talks about."

"So? He's adaptable, as he must be, seeing that he's at the mercy of the world," I said.

But Thomas, with his indifferent expression, felt like a closed door. He'd made up his mind about Ben, summed him up in a neat, tidy sentence. With Thomas, it had to be the right moment, he had to be in the right mood, or he was impenetrable. As if to prove my point, he left the room. Then I heard the hiss of the shower.

✳   ✳   ✳

When Ben showed up the next time, Thomas was home and they went outside to shoot baskets. I watched from the window. Having gone to so many of Thomas's games over the years, I knew you could learn a lot about a person by how they played basketball. Thomas was shooting threes. He practiced that shot religiously, transferring it into points in a game. Guarding Thomas, working to get the rebounds, Ben looked older, more muscular. He, too, shot from far away. Thomas was on the basketball team; Ben was not. Ben didn't make a single shot, so I revised my thinking about him: risk-taker, reckless. But maybe not. I thought about what Thomas had said; maybe Ben was a pleaser.

I left the window and went to my desk, thinking I'd write something, but I couldn't focus. I went back to the kitchen and started snapping green beans.

Thomas came into the house.

"Where's Ben?"

"He went home. Or so he said. He probably went to someone else's house because I said I had a lot of homework and couldn't hang out."

I set the spatula down.

Thomas looked at me, sweat trickling down his red face. "Mom, he's kind of a creep."

"Why do you say that?"

He opened the fridge, pulled out the pitcher of water. "He said you're really nice and smart, and you're a pleasure to talk to. Who says stuff like that?"

A young man who hadn't contorted and twisted himself into the conventional fifteen-year-old. A young man who was his own person. A young man who was self-assured and confident, achieving what, for most people, took years. I was about to say all that to Thomas, but he spoke first.

"And," he said, taking a deep breath, "he said you're good-looking."

My face felt hot. Ben didn't seem like the macho type, trying to impress Thomas with talk like that. I was embarrassed, then flattered, then embarrassed again that I felt anything at all.

"It's misplaced affection for his mother," I said.

Thomas raised an eyebrow. "Calling you good-looking?'"

Grease splattered and burned my wrist. "Have you met his mother?"

He set down his glass. "Why are you being so nice to him?"

"Why are you asking?"

"It seems you're going out of your way to be nice to him." He scoffed. "It's so typical of you."

I turned off the stove, but the flame sputtered and continued to burn. "Which is what?"

"Just trying to make up for all the times you aren't nice."

I wasn't sure what he was thinking about, but suspected it had something to do with a $100 jacket he wanted. I'd said he'd have to wait until Christmas.

"The jacket?" I said. "Are we back to that?"

"Just forget it. I don't want to be friends with him."

"So if he shows up, I send him away? I'd say you're being harsh."

He didn't say anything. Then: "Dad. You weren't nice to him in the end."

His voice quivered, as if he'd suffered an irreparable loss, and in that moment, I glimpsed Thomas's former young self, the boy who wept when his hamster died. Together we held a proper funeral in the backyard. All at once, I felt I'd made a terrible mistake, not just how I'd handled the divorce, but everything, the way I'd chosen to live, make a living, raise Thomas, as if at every turn, I'd opted to take the wrong direction, though I couldn't say what was the right direction.

Thomas shook his head. "Forget it."

He left. Music blared from his room, creating a sonic wall.

✻   ✻   ✻

The next time Ben came over, Thomas wasn't home. We sat in the living room, drinking ice tea, talking about D. H. Lawrence, Faulkner,

Hemingway, and Carver.

I got up and handed him Woolf's *To the Lighthouse*. "You have to read it."

He looked at me closely. "It's one of your favorites, isn't it?"

"I read it every year."

He looked at the cover, turned it over and read the back, then turned it back to the cover, a picture of a woman lit by the sun, which he stroked as if it were a precious thing.

"You must read a lot," he said.

I sat down on the couch next to him. "I often find it more pleasurable to read than be with people."

"Me, too."

"There are days when I don't want to venture out, the world seems it's become the devil's, all evidence of God's existence banished."

He raised an eyebrow. "You're religious?"

"No, though I wish I was. All those ready-made answers."

He nodded solemnly and looked at the glass of ice tea in his hand. He said he'd read Dante's *Inferno* a couple months ago, hoping to make sense of the world, but it only made him more confused. "I don't feel like I have any answers."

The sweep of his hair fell loosely in a fan across his forehead.

I laughed. "Really? You're one of the most poised and aware young men I've met in a long time. Thomas could learn a lot from you."

He laughed bitterly at that. "I doubt it. He's pretty self-assured, you know."

If he meant impenetrable, like a door slammed shut, holding me back like an eager dog, he was right.

The night Ben had spent here, I'd given him a toothbrush. I got up now and retrieved it from the bathroom. I put it in a plastic Ziploc bag for him. He laughed. "Maybe I should keep it here. You never know when I might get locked out again."

Somehow the way he said it sounded sexual, and I realized I was standing quite close to him. If he moved his knee, he'd brush against my leg.

"No, take it," I said, stepping back.

He slipped it into his backpack. He opened the Woolf book and read the opening. He looked at me, his eyes bright, shiny. "I can tell I'm going to love it."

✻   ✻   ✻

The next day at work, one of my colleagues plopped herself in the chair in my office and talked about all the sacrifices she'd made for her children. She'd given up oil painting; she used to ride her bike every day, now she was lucky to ride once a week and, as a result, she'd put on twenty pounds. Her best friend—she rarely saw her anymore. "I'm pared down so far, I'm skin and bones, metaphorically, of course." She didn't recognize herself. But the crazy thing was she couldn't stop herself from paring herself down even more—she had no time to reflect, no time to think, between work and three children and a husband, she was completely absorbed in the act of living day-to-day. Every time she thought about going away, just her, a spa or retreat or something, she imagined her children, going to bed too late, waking up, eating whatever they found in a cupboard.

When I pulled into the driveway, Ben was sitting on the steps. As I got closer, I saw he was dirty.

"Locked out again?" I said.

He nodded. A smudge of dirt was on his cheek like a gash. Had he slept outside? Under a tree or on a bench somewhere? I felt a wave of tenderness come over me, and as I opened the front door, he followed me in. After I shut the door, I turned, and he was right there, right in front of me. He had a faint freckle below his left eyebrow. His eyes shiny, excited, and he was so close, I could see streaks of hazel in his eyes and smell his sweat. He took hold of my hand, tightened his grip, then pressed me against the wall and kissed me hard on the lips.

I yanked my hand back, stepped away. "What do you think you're doing?"

After my rush of anger, there was something I hadn't counted on: I hadn't expected there to be anything fearful in his sheepishness. He hung his head, his chin tucked into his neck. I could feel the quiver of his fear. Before he uttered a word, I said, "That was not necessary." It was my tone that surprised me now—kind, as if I understood such things happened and the world could contain them.

It must have been this sentiment that made me step aside and allow him to come in—a more magnanimous, more generous me. He sat at the table, and, not looking at me, fidgeted with the salt and pepper shakers.

"Why did you do that?" I said.

I wanted to have one of our honest conversations, but he didn't say anything. He looked worn out. Deep purple bags under his eyes, heavy eyelids.

Out of habit, I began fixing him a sandwich. I opened a cupboard, pulled out two glasses, and when I turned, he was gone. I hadn't heard the front door open or close. Did he leave? Was he somewhere in the house? Thomas wouldn't be home for several hours. Basketball practice, then out to dinner with friends. There were signs he had a girlfriend, and though he hadn't said anything, I'd heard actual conversations on the phone with his door closed. Long conversations, the steady pulse of his new low voice, even laughter, genuine laughter, which I hadn't heard in a long time.

"Ben?" I said.

I stood still in the kitchen, listening for him.

"Ben," I said, louder this time.

Was he playing a game? Hide and seek? What if his clothes were strewn on my floor, and he was naked in my bed? The house was still. Sunlight poured in through the big windows, and a dog was barking somewhere in the neighborhood, a steady bark, as if trying to remind its owners it still existed.

I grew up in a house on a lake, and in the summer, before the speedboats and wind, the water was pure glass. I'd head down to the dock and dive in, sculpting thousands of ripples, causing the dock to gently rise and fall, the small silver fish to scatter. It would be shockingly cold, but I'd swim hard and fast, smooth, powerful strokes, and soon the water would be perfect. I'd swim to the buoy, about a hundred yards from the shore, and tread water, and from there, I'd see our house on the hill, the hill of green grass like a carpet, my bedroom window on the first floor with the light blue curtains with small white flowers. I'd imagine myself in my bedroom, looking at myself in the lake, and it felt like I was seeing my two lives, the girl standing in the bedroom, the one who did her chores and homework and was praised for her proper manners and quiet presence and good grades, and the girl in the lake, who was another person altogether. Who didn't care about proper and polite, who rumbled with rage and jealousy and ambition, who, when Ben held her hand, kissed her, felt a flicker of desire, the excitement of being desired, desirable.

The house's silence pressed in on me. "Ben?" I said, quieter this time.

He wasn't in Thomas's bedroom, nor in mine. I went into the living room. A lump on the couch. He was lying on his side, asleep. He looked so vulnerable, so young, so emptied out.

I shook his shoulder, waking him.

He stirred, startled, sat up.

"You should go now," I said.

He looked at me, bewildered.

"Go."

He looked at me intently, as if hunting for something, a deeper meaning of what I'd just said. Then, he left.

For a long time, I stood there. When Thomas came home, I didn't mention that Ben had been here or what had happened.

Halloween came and went. Thanksgiving, and Thomas had his two best friends over, and I invited a colleague who lived alone. After the shock of that afternoon, then came a sense of my complicity, and, with that, shame. I was relieved Ben stopped coming to our house, and at the same time, I wanted him to stop by so I could apologize. Once, as I was driving home from work, I thought I saw him. A hoodie on, the same slope to his shoulders, the same height. I sped up, and when I reached him, slowed down, ready to roll down the window, ask if he needed a ride, food, anything. It wasn't him.

The next time I saw him, it was months later. He was with another boy, walking beside him, talking and laughing. I still remembered the taste of him in my mouth. He saw me, as I slowed, but he didn't wave and his blank face suggested he didn't recognize me. He was heading the opposite direction of my house. ❧

Nina Schuyler is the author of the novels The Translator *(Pegasus Books) and* The Painting *(Algonquin Books), a finalist for the Northern California Book Award, and lives in San Anselmo, California.*

SELFIES

KEVIN SIMMONDS

No tumors yet
exposure
after exposure
angling for that vantage yet
plain flat yet
in relief

elbow wrist & finger
joint effort

what's left / out

*

You swipe

scrutinize for a face that jives

with the prescription

bystanders should have

of your features

so you can feature less

more

until each frame contains the same

shot

muscle memory of pout

& squint

head tilt

& lilt

You do this

with your finger

like smoothing wrinkles or wiping dust

from a screen preening

to be seen

UPON SEEING AN OLD PHOTO OF SYLVESTER

KEVIN SIMMONDS

Girl you
foretold the harsh lighting
of *RuPaul's Drag Race* Season One
giving us glamazon headshot realness
10s across the board

I'm in the queer archives
black sweater
another seer's name in red
across my chest
         Basquiat
drop crotch pants from Shibuya
& slip-ons in magenta

Magenta
an extra-spectral color: it cannot
be generated by light of a single wavelength

Magenta you
equal parts red & blue
midway between Violet & Rose
But your drag name would be more legendary

Prayer beads of your falsetto
the anal beads
how you took church out
the church
for all us backsliders

for real
in your leather
for real
in your turban & robes
prophesying life of the world
to come

*

Falsetto

    : noun

singing that enables the singer to sing notes
beyond the normal range

sound produced by the vibration of the ligament edges
of the vocal cords

Ligament

    : noun

tough & flexible connective tissue

Sylvester

    : name derived from the Latin adjective *silvestris*
    meaning *wooded* or *wild*

*

Tell us what to do
Now that we've given up wilding
    for wedding registries
    circuit cruises
    quartz countertops & volunteering
    for the military

Never mind the countless invisible infected
by the virus still
      mostly black

the genderless & gender-defiant
slain because they're from the future
      mostly colored

All the while we lip-synch Beyoncé
      like a Negro spiritual

    *

We bond around trauma
around vendetta
blindingly tribal
on our phones
on our feeds
at our brunches
& our marches

We police like the republic polices

      hunker down

      on keys

      to scream

      the platform

      into action

unwilling to seek
what's real
we race to the scene to see
who can be more righteous
& aggrieved
& worthy to hand down

the punishing judgment

*

What'll blind us
so we can see
that what binds us
is more than air
or who we fuck
or who wants to erase us

Us who act out
of anger
of hurt
of rage
of fear
& bound
with might
to empty
the page
          first
of sentences
               then
of lines

Kevin Simmonds is the author of the poetry collections Bend to It *(Salmon Poetry) and* Mad for Meat *(Salmon Poetry), and lives in San Francisco.*

DESIRE, TEXT, AND A SAN FRANCISCO APARTMENT
INTERVIEW WITH DODIE BELLAMY AND KEVIN KILLIAN

DANIEL BENJAMIN

I sat down with authors and artists Dodie Bellamy and the late Kevin Killian in their Minna Street apartment in San Francisco on a Sunday afternoon in early May. I didn't know it would be my last time seeing Kevin—he died following complications from chemotherapy on June 15, 2019. On the day of my visit, Kevin was in high spirits, even though he and Dodie had recently returned from a hospital stay following his cancer diagnosis. Kevin was enthusiastic about ongoing projects, and seemed to be speeding up more than slowing down.

In tributes to Kevin following his death, many writers have noted the various forms of mentorship by which he and Dodie supported them, and more generally, the Bay Area's writing and art scenes. Dodie has frequently run a writing workshop in their home, in which Kevin was an active participant. The two co-edited *Mirage #4/Period(ical)* for many years, a Xerox publication that put many poets into print for the first time. Kevin hosted dozens of readings at Alley Cat Books in San Francisco's Mission District, often bringing together more established local poets with younger visiting writers, introducing them to the San Francisco scene. In more formal contexts, the two regularly taught at San Francisco State University, California College of the Arts, and other schools in the Bay Area. And through his work as the literary executor of the revered Bay Area poet Jack Spicer, Kevin guided many scholars and publishers.

That is how I came to know Kevin: before moving to the Bay Area for graduate school in 2012, I found his email address and wrote to him, asking for details about an unpublished Spicer fragment he described in an article. He quickly wrote back, sending the full story, encouraging me to look him up when I moved here, and promising I would have a "thrill ride" looking at the Spicer notebooks myself. Always happy to discuss an archival mystery and to work out various interpretations of a given work, Kevin was something of an informal adviser to my doctorate work on Spicer.

In the seventies, a circle of queer writers coalesced in San Francisco, taking energies from critical theory, innovative poetry, and the feminist and queer political struggles of the preceding decades, and formed the New Narrative movement. Kevin and Dodie were at its center. As they write at the start of *Writers Who Love Too Much: New Narrative Writing 1977–1997* (Nightboat Books, 2017), their recent anthology of the subject:

> Founded in the San Francisco poetry scene of the late 1970s, New Narrative responded to post-structuralist quarrels with traditional storytelling practice for reinscribing "master narrative," and attempted to open up the field to a wider range of subjects … It would be a writing prompted not by fiat nor consensus, nor by the totalizing suggestions of the MFA "program era," but by community; it would be unafraid of experiment, unafraid of kitsch, unafraid of sex and gossip and political debate.

144 Novice writers have been lectured since forever to "show, don't tell," but one thing New Narrative did was tell and tell and tell without the cheap obscurantism of "showing." (i)

The movement began in workshops run by Robert Glück at Small Press Traffic, then a bookstore in Noe Valley that featured inexpensive, limited-run publications lacking formal methods of distribution. (Small Press Traffic operates to this day, hosting readings, running workshops, and offering residencies. In the 1990s, Dodie was its director.) With support from the California Arts Council, Glück ran three separate workshops: one for older writers, one for gay men, and one for all comers. The "general" workshop became the incubator for New Narrative writing. Participants included Bruce Boone, Camille Roy, Steve Abbott, Francesca Rosa, Michael Amnasan, Marsha Campbell, Sam D'Allesandro, and Gabrielle Daniels. When Bellamy and Killian arrived in San Francisco in the early 1980s, New Narrative was already on its way. In their anthology's introduction, they offer a vivid picture of this moment, and of Glück's teaching method that brought together high theory with works of popular culture.

Dodie and Kevin met in the workshop—Bellamy from Chicago, Killian from New York. They married in 1986. Dodie has written of their "mixed marriage," Kevin being a gay man and she having previously been involved with both men and women:

> Reading Kevin and other gay authors, I saw how erotic writing could be more than just a description of sexual acts. It could create a new sexual relationship: the writer as top, the reader as bottom. Sexuality is far more fluid for my queer compadres than it was for gay men I knew in college, who would never dare touch—or admit to touching—a woman. But everything is different in San Francisco. One queer friend told me that

when he had sex with a woman and pretended to be straight, **145**
it was dreadful—but when he had straight sex as a gay man
it was a lot of fun.

Several of their works emerge out of this moment. Dodie's novel *The Letters of Mina Harker* (1998) combines pastiche of Bram Stoker's *Dracula* with letters to real-life interlocutors, crossing the boundaries between art and life. Kevin's memoir *Bedrooms Have Windows* (1989), recently republished by Semiotexte in *Fascination* (2018), plumbs the various and contradictory valences of sexual and artistic formation.

In many ways, New Narrative describes a highly specific moment in time and space. These writers were responding to the Language poets—such as Lyn Hejinian, Barrett Watten, Ron Silliman, and Carla Harryman—who had emerged in the 1970s and published magazines, hosted readings and talks, and played increasingly prominent roles in Bay Area's poetry institutions. (The Language poets brought a theoretically intensive study of Russian formalism, Marxism, and deconstruction into the conversation; their writing tended to focus on rigorous formal experimentation while eschewing narrative.) But New Narrative also followed previous generations of queer San Francisco writing, and belongs to the moment after the political struggles of the 1960s and before the horrific losses of the HIV/AIDS epidemic.

The movement's impact can be felt across Bay Area writing today in the work of poets and experimental prose writers such as Renee Gladman, Rob Halpern, Pamela Lu, and Jocelyn Saidenberg, who have worked with New Narrative's original practitioners, recasting and developing some of its methods. All the while, Kevin and Dodie have played a prominent role in this continuing history as teachers, publishers, and community pillars, passing on the gift of New Narrative, perhaps one of the "gifts of San Francisco" Kevin details in a poem from his final collection, *Tony Greene Era* (2017). The poem recounts the local origins

146 of (among other things) the Popsicle, the Mai Tai, the fortune cookie, and the It's-It:

> ... *graham crackers and chocolate, dipped over ice cream,*
> *part time paradise, like its id, and these,*
>
> *the gifts of San Francisco, I extend to the ego, the superego,*
> *the colors and germs of your generosity.*

The movement's influence extends beyond San Francisco, too. Kathy Acker, Dennis Cooper, Chris Kraus, and Eileen Myles show connections to New Narrative, appearing in the same publications, and similarly combining autobiography, theory, and fiction. More recently, writers of "autofictions" such as Ben Lerner and Sheila Heti, show the effects of New Narrative, even if they would not necessarily recognize themselves in its lineage.

While *The Letters of Mina Harker* and *Bedrooms Have Windows* are essential New Narrative texts, the span of Kevin Killian and Dodie Bellamy's works—biography, collections of poetry, stories, essays, and novels—shows how variously the movement resonates, in a great variety of forms. And together and separately, they have published copious amounts of art criticism and built deep connections with the visual and performing arts, including curating an exhibition at the di Rosa Center for Contemporary Art in 2018 and producing art of their own. (Killian's *Tagged* series of photographs poses artists, writers, and academics with a drawing of male genitalia by Raymond Pettibon; Bellamy's work combining photography and found objects has appeared at galleries in Oakland and Bellingham, Washington. And this year, the Wattis Institute for Contemporary Art's "research season" has focused on Dodie, with a series of readings, performances, and talks centering around her work and its impact.)

I talked to Dodie and Kevin about their anthology, which has done much to record New Narrative work for posterity. And while some New Narrative authors have sizable if cult followings, the anthology also amplifies writers who might otherwise fade from view, such as Marsha Campbell, Lawrence Braithwaite, and many others. In all, *Writers Who Love Too Much* raises fascinating questions regarding the nature of an avant-garde and the status of San Francisco writing today.

Before I left their apartment that day, Kevin walked over to a dresser and pulled out an old and battered briefcase. It had belonged, he said, to Frank O'Hara. He removed from it a few broadsides from the 1960s that they already had in duplicate (with all the art on the walls, sometimes stacked four or five paintings deep, there wasn't even room to display work they only had one copy of), and he sent me home with two of them. This kind of generous act was typical of Kevin. In the days since his death, I've been thinking about the love he gave so generously—to San Francisco, to writers and artists, and to the world, but primarily to Dodie. Community was important to Kevin, and his partnership with Dodie the most important of all.

—July 2019

DANIEL BENJAMIN (DB): In the introduction to *Writers Who Love Too Much*, you state, "The heroic age of New Narrative had already come and gone by the time that the two of us arrived in San Francisco, Dodie from Chicago, Kevin from Long Island. Dodie came to Bob's workshop at the suggestion of the poet Kathleen Fraser, from whom she was auditing grad poetry classes at San Francisco State University on the outskirts of town. And Kevin lived a few blocks away and had stuck his head in the bookstore a few times before noticing the signs in the hallway, 'Free Weekly Writing Workshop'... As soon as we joined, we entered a bustling world of continuous edu-

148 cation. Everyone went to the same readings and parties and lectures and the same movies." What drew you to San Francisco from Long Island and Chicago—what made you come here in the first place?

DODIE BELLAMY: I had been here at a conference a few years before-hand and, coming from Indiana, I was in a long-term lesbian rela-tionship at the time. Just seeing gay people and giant strawberries on the street, I really liked it. And then I moved to Chicago after col-lege and broke up with my long-term girlfriend, and all my gay boy-friends from college had moved to San Francisco. So I moved out here because they found me a job. They put me up, they found me an apartment, and it was really easy. I had a social world to start with. It was very random. I had no idea there was a writing scene. It was really the best place in the world for me to go because I was always wanting to be a writer but never really making that commitment.

I had very little money. I had like $600. The first thing I bought before I got an apartment was a stereo. [Laughter] This was a girl who had no sense of how the real world operates. But the people I bought the stereo from, I took their apartment, too, because they were moving. And then I also took their dishes. So it worked out.

DB: Where was your first apartment?

DODIE: It was on Pine Street, I think. I didn't stay there long, but my best friend took it over. So I went back to it a lot—Pine between Van Ness and Polk.

DB: How did you first get into Kathleen's workshop and start going to readings?

DODIE: I just started going to readings. I would go to readings from the Poetry Flash; that was where everything was listed. I would just go, because I was re-ally interested, and I saw a lot of incredible things. And I was in-volved with the Feminist Writers' Guild, and a friend of mine in the Feminist Writers' Guild suggested I take Kathleen's workshop. That's how that happened. I took four classes with her and then she suggested Bob [Glück]'s workshop. Her class ended in the afternoon, and she would actually drive me from San Francisco State to Bob's workshop. And Marcia Campbell sometimes would come as well. So all the women in New Narrative—Marcia [Campbell], Megan [Camille Roy], and I all came from Kathleen's suggestions. So she really took it from male homosexuals to kind of a more female presence. And then there was Francesca Rosa.

KEVIN KILLIAN: But I like the angle that you were denied entry into the MFA [at San Francisco State], you couldn't get into the—

DODIE: No, at a certain point I applied for—they didn't have an MFA program then, it was just an MA. I applied to the grad writing program and got rejected. [Laughter]

Kathleen then went and lobbied on my behalf and got me accepted. But then I decided, stupidly, that I already had two master's degrees. Why did I want another one? I didn't realize that I would actually end up teaching writing.

DB: Kevin, in one of your memoirs, you tell the story about leaving a Ted Berrigan reading with pockets full of pills and getting in a car and driving out West. Is that how it happened?

KEVIN: I was writing my dissertation, like you, and I had finished my coursework and I was kind of having a breakdown. So my sister, who lived here in San Francisco, had an extra room in her apartment, and she said, "Come and finish your thing here, you wouldn't even have to pay rent." I wanted to return to San Francisco so I came to her place.

It was a different world for both of us, I think, because we didn't know it, but these apartments were dirt-cheap and they were widely available. I don't even think anybody has an extra room now. What my sister was offering, it doesn't exist as a concept now.

DB: Where was the apartment?

KEVIN: Guerrero at 24th Street. It was between the Mission and Noe Valley.

150

DODIE: That's how we started getting involved. I moved to Bartlett Street, which was just a couple of blocks down. So we started hanging out all the time because we were so close to each other.

KEVIN: It was close to the workshop, where Small Press Traffic was, on 24th and Elizabeth. Dodie was the genius when I walked in. She was already kind of established.

DODIE: We're talking months or a year, maybe. I was in it a little longer.

KEVIN: I also went through the Poetry Flash thing, but this one was free. You didn't have to pay anything. It was all paid for by the California Arts Council.

DODIE: And the NEA.

KEVIN: Yes. And so they hired Bob to do three classes a week, with the different constituencies. And one was a gay class—gay men, I guess.

"It wasn't until 1980 when Reagan was elected that everything changed. So we got to see the last dregs of that kind of energy."

DODIE: Yeah, they wouldn't let me in it.

KEVIN: And there was one for seniors on Saturdays, and then there was the one where Dodie and I worked together first. It's like that was the New Narrative workshop.

DODIE: The different workshops interacted a lot and hung out together.

KEVIN: It was kind of a gay scene and, plus, why I came was, you know, it was for the boys. It was the age before AIDS. I don't know how you would experience it, Dodie, but for men it was this sexual paradise. Maybe not as exciting as the one in New York, which was very, very dangerous and creepy, but it was like a hippie heaven.

DODIE: I moved here in the late seventies and it still had that hippie edge. It wasn't until 1980 when Reagan was elected that everything changed. So we got to see the last dregs of that kind of energy.

KEVIN: But San Francisco was also falling apart when Dodie moved here. Jonestown [Massacre] happened, Harvey Milk was assassinated, and Patty Hearst was kidnapped. It was like every day there'd be some, like, apocalyptic thing.

DODIE: But then Armistead Maupin's *Tales of the City* was serialized in the paper, too.

KEVIN: *Tales of the City* drew me here!

DB: Kevin, what got you into Jack Spicer? I'm curious how that affected your experience of living here, going deep into the history of a previous generation?

KEVIN: I had been warned by one of the professors in my PhD program, "Sure, there's a lot of writing in San Francisco, but there's a lot of gay people out there who will take advantage of boys." And I'm like, what? [Laughter] One of them had written a book partly about Robert Duncan, so he said, "Go with Duncan. But there was this hideous, evil man called Jack Spicer, who luckily died. You want to get out of that scene. It's demonic." That intrigued me. When I went into Bob's workshop, we met Lew Ellingham, who was in the class. And Lew had just come out of an alcoholic funk and was living homeless in Golden Gate Park.

He was part of some 12-step program, and I think one of the things you do is just try to do something big and grand that your habit had prevented you from. So that was Lew's idea, he was going to interview all the people who knew Spicer and write an oral history. And that's where I said, "I don't know much about Spicer." And Bob said, "Well, then come sit down between us."

It was only fifteen years since Spicer's death. So some of the people we were interviewing were our age now.

DODIE: It felt like so long ago. But yes, it wasn't that long.

KEVIN: Now all those people would be ninety; then they were forty, maybe fifty. There were a

152 lot of survivors, and thank God Lew started this work before I joined his team because he interviewed Duncan for days. And if that wasn't in our book, our book wouldn't have been so fantastic.

You probably heard the story of how Lew had worked on this for eight years, and he was getting some interest from Cal and places like that, publishing these different interviews in high-class places. But nobody wanted to actually publish the manuscript he had produced because it was all drawn up according to what he thought were Spicer lines. Leave in all the mistakes, leave all the *uhs* and *buts*. People never finished a sentence in those days.

Lew only focused on the last seven years of Jack's life because that's the time during which he knew him. So he kind of accidentally picked up other things from earlier periods of his life, but people just really wanted to have a biography of Spicer. Lew came to me because I had written a novel, so I knew something about narrative. And I said, "Yeah, I could do this." And the advantage to the project, in general, was that not everybody liked Lew and not everybody would speak with him, so I could be like a fresh face.

DODIE: Kevin charmed a lot of hostile people into talking to him.

KEVIN: I was ruthless. They said, "I'll talk to you if you're straight." I'm straight! "I can only talk to another gay man about this." Well, I'm gay! I think I spoke about that to Dodie's class one time, the ruthlessness of the biographer. And I've always loved biographies.

DB: So shortly after coming here, you became a historian of the Bay Area poetry scene.

KEVIN: I got to know a lot about Spicer and was blown away by the work. And I was like, "Why doesn't everybody write like this? Why are all these people wasting time with Language poetry?" But there was a great convergence at that moment of all the different schools in the '80s. New College events? They were all there. Everybody agreed: Spicer was the great king of writing.

DB: In the introduction you talk about how you had been involved in other scenes before New Narrative, and how New Narrative had connections to the New York School, the Berkeley Renaissance (comprised of Spicer, Duncan, and Robin Blaser), the Harlem Renaissance, and other "queer-fueled avant-gardes." And I found an interview, Dodie, where you say New Narrative is like a cult. Do you think New Narrative is like these other movements?

DODIE: Well, in some ways, the fact that it had these teachers and these authorities rather than a group of peers coming together, it's almost like it was kind of looking forward to the MFA system. We were like students. But I think that a lot of social groupings are cult-like, like the Marxist poets that are so much into—Marxists are often in cults, political cults.

KEVIN: Even today! But it seemed clear that Bob and Bruce Boone had studied the success of the Language poets and decided

we should imitate them as much as possible.

DODIE: But the Language poets, again, were a peer-based group. Their problem was that they wouldn't allow any—

KEVIN: They didn't want any students!

DODIE: People would try to become one of them, and they'd just push them out.

DB: But Bob and Bruce were looking for acolytes.

DODIE: I think the reason why we got treated so well is that we weren't Bob and Bruce, who they had issues with and criticized. But we weren't trying to be Language poets, either. So actually we can't really complain about our period. Barrett Watten was really supportive of me. And Carla [Harryman] was supportive of us.

KEVIN: It partly was because of the intense reaction Language poets had produced in the Bay Area writing community. People hated them and their ruthless domination.

DODIE: And I can't believe that

154 hatred is still going on.

DB: Dodie, I was looking at your website and you described *The Letters of Mina Harker* as the book that taught you how to write. I'm curious to hear you elaborate on that.

DODIE: When I went into Bob's workshop, I was still a poet. But I'd always been drawn to narrative. Narrative poetry was just, you weren't gonna do it in 1980s San Francisco.

KEVIN: It was like the newspaper at the bottom of the hamster cage.

DODIE: So I learned a way to write narrative in that workshop where you could still have all the kinds of candy that poetry would give you. Narrative in prose was this sort of foreign land to me. And so I really didn't know there's a different type of music to prose and the way it works. So I literally learned how to write prose with that book. It started out as this casual project. The first seventy-five pages of the original manuscript became the first ten pages. I really shaped it. Kevin's very good at shaping, so

he helped a lot, too.

Each of those letters, particularly the later ones, would take a month to write. I'd really spend a lot of time. And it's kind of a baroque book. I was trying to pull out all the stops. I think I still do all the same things in my writing that I do in that book, but they're done much more subtly and maybe not as intensely. Kind of more spread out. I don't know. Do you think that book works still?

DB: I do, and when I was thinking of this interview, I was thinking about it as being in conversation with the Spicer work Kevin was doing at the time, in that there's an attempt to map a network. Not through the traditional way of understanding it, but through desire, through text, and through objects.

DODIE: My motivation was that I was really finding writing exciting, but I was kind of bored by my life. So it was a way to incorporate the life into the writing and add that edge, because I was constantly not only crossing boundaries in the writing, I was purposely sending people letters that were inappropriate and crossing social boundaries. So that was kind of scary and exciting at the same time.

KEVIN: I would add, Dodie, that one of our arguments about New Narrative in *Writers Who Love Too Much* is that all of us were poets who had to turn to prose at that moment because poetry was not sufficient. Poetry was not sufficient to convey the reality and the nightmare of those times.

DODIE: Successful poetry to me is creating an experience, and isn't necessarily conveying information in a direct way. But also we weren't writing "poetic," we weren't doing Michael Ondaatje, you know what I mean? Where the prose becomes so poetic? And in fact there was an attempt to be kind of vulgar and coarse, and that was an antipoetic thrust in some ways.

KEVIN: Well, it was a great age for horror. Horror was everything in the '80s.

DODIE: And also writing that made people uncomfortable and showed them what they didn't want to look at.

DB: When I think about people like you, as well as the New Narrative conference, I get an image of San Francisco as a beacon. A place people are coming to and that is sending writing and art and ways of writing out around the world. Do you think there's still a San Francisco scene that is comparable to other scenes garnering attention?

KEVIN: I don't think there is a San Francisco scene because of the politics of economics. There's no way young people can survive here.

The other answer is that our methods, which seem so radical and revolutionary, are now what they teach in MFA programs! Autofiction…

DODIE: Not the ones that I teach in!

> *"Poetry was not sufficient to convey the reality and the nightmare of those times."*

156 **DB:** Yeah, like Ben Lerner.

KEVIN: Maggie Nelson. These people are the writers being taught, and they're doing what we did. And that's so gratifying, in a way.

KEVIN: The rise of the Internet changed everything. People blogging—there is no more authority.

DODIE: The Internet has also helped make the culture much stupider than it was before. It's weird to grow old in an environment that's more conservative than what you were raised in.

DB: I'm thirty-one. I talk to students who are nineteen and they don't have a sense of a future, they don't have a belief—

DODIE: It would be hard to. Don't you even think that with the Mueller Report, it seems like there's this new layer of despair?

DB: Yes. It's like, what could they say? Nothing would change.

KEVIN: Even Dodie, Rachel Maddow's greatest fan, just stopped watching her!

DODIE: It's not her fault!

DB: Dodie, in your essay "In the Shadow of Twitter Towers," you have this motif of talking about San Francisco as a "bad place," citing Stephen King. I was drawn to the passage where you wrote, "A bad place doesn't spring up on its own. Something creates it. Atrocity births ghosts; soulless gentrification herds the desperate into ghettos away from moneyed eyes of tourists."

DODIE: Well, that's changed, right? They're right in front of the tourists now.

DB: When you write, "atrocity births ghosts," do you see a connection between the losses of the AIDS epidemic and the current disaster of tech gentrification?

KEVIN: That's Sarah Schulman's argument, right? That AIDS led to people losing their apartments, death, mass death, and speculators moving in and taking advantage of that. So hideous. But to me it's kind of convincing, and it did happen here as well as in New York.

DB: In your essay, Dodie, it almost feels like an eerie, ghostly repetition. Like the dead are wandering around San Francisco.

DODIE: I was also influenced by *Our Lady of Darkness* by Fritz Leiber. That book really set the tone for the essay. Who would think that you can write a novel where gentrification is the monster? I think just living in a space for a long time, everywhere you go, things that were there are no longer. Now it's more rapid than before. I go to a neighborhood and I often feel memories or nostalgia, but also this sense of loss. And you know, sometimes it feels like I mourn my past as if it were a death.

Everyone talks about how the vibrancy of the city, and a place for alternate ways of life, is just diminished. It's hardly here anymore. I mean there are pockets of it still, but there's not very much of it. I guess the alternative way of life here would be homelessness, but nobody wants that experience.

DB: Kevin, in your recent poetry books, the work of memorializing those lost to AIDS seems as present as ever. I'm thinking most recently of *Tony Greene Era*. In the poem at the end of that book, you write, "What I could see coming was that/I'd be here reading for you still,/today, late at night in San Francisco." What does it mean to still be writing in the wake of the epidemic and the relevance of that memory work today?

KEVIN: AIDS was the epochal event in my life. Not that I have AIDS or anything like that, but we were in the center of a wonderful world, not only of pleasure, but of society, and the curtain came down on it. And what do you do with that? Well, it did politicize me to a degree. And I began seeing the bigger picture of things, and that angered me, so it went into protests and so forth. But it also made me question the validity of art and writing in

> *"Everyone talks about how the vibrancy of the city, and a place for alternate ways of life, is just diminished. It's hardly here anymore."*

158

the face of a huge social injustice.

DODIE: I think that's been going on a lot here now, too. You have to constantly keep evaluating if it's worthwhile to write, especially with no sense of future. Like when we sold our archives, that came up a lot. It seems silly to put something in an archive if you don't believe that it's even going to exist.

do something. A leveling kind of death like AIDS showed me that all art was connected with each other. It wasn't just about our writing scene. It was about music, cinema, visual art. And those were things in which I began to take a great deal more interest at that time, and I think Dodie, too.

My idea about *The Letters of*

> "*A leveling kind of death like* AIDS *showed me that all art was connected with each other. It wasn't just about our writing scene. It was about music, cinema, visual art.*"

KEVIN: I couldn't write about AIDS while it was happening.

DODIE: He was terrified.

KEVIN: It always seemed like it was the wrong thing to do, morally.

DODIE: But then, for a lot of writers, there was a political imperative to write about AIDS. Until it became like a cliché, like "There they are with their AIDS poem."

KEVIN: As you know I found a way out of it, but it was after the drug cocktails. I said, now I can

Mina Harker, which I watched Dodie write, was that what was so unique about it was that she wasn't just writing to Dennis [Cooper] and so forth, she was writing to William Gibson, to visual artists, to all kinds of people in all different disciplines. Partly, that was encouraged by Bob.

DODIE: I would say, though, that our connection to the larger art world came much more through Dennis, because he literally introduced us to an incredible scene in L.A.

KEVIN: And Kathy Acker also had that. She was involved in so many different things. Those kind of people made the New Narrative "strict" scene seem like tending your own garden.

DODIE: Provincial?

KEVIN: Yes. Which was the goal, I think, of New Narrative—to work on your own backyard!

DODIE: I still believe that things that are small and local often are purer than things that are popular. Having to teach in fiction programs—

KEVIN: Where everything has to be universal—

DODIE: If it has a *New York Times* review, then it's valid. Whereas I don't have that belief that something that doesn't attain that is a failure. In fact, I believe the opposite.

DB: I have one more question on the hyperlocal, which is—this apartment! In your writing, Dodie, you talk about all the changes in the neighborhood, and I think a lot

of people in San Francisco today talk about what it's like being in a rent-controlled apartment and having everything change around them and being unable to leave because you can't afford to move.

But you were also saying, Kevin, that you're having someone catalog the paintings here—and every time I step in here, it's so special because the communities that you've gathered around you are really bursting off the walls. What is this space like for you? Could you maybe tell me about any pieces in particular that feel like part of your life here?

DODIE: Well, we both feel like there's too much stuff. We feel buried in stuff and we want to get rid of it! And we have made various attempts that kind of sputter out.

KEVIN: But now we can put that into usage, I think—our artwork did not go with our literary archives. And that was a clear indication of how it's still true: writers can't make money. Artists can, and art collectors! And it's possible we could live on the things that came to us, that people gave, or that we paid $50 a month for. And that made me think, God, how much money did I make last year on writing? Probably under $10,000.

DODIE: But all the money that you did make on writing was probably art related.

KEVIN: Exactly! That was Eileen [Myles]'s lesson, and Dennis's, too.

DODIE: I've been making more money than ever on writing, but it's all on art.

DB: It goes back even to Ashbery, who made a living on art writing before he could on his poetry.

DODIE: I don't know that I could make a living on it, but it's nice. I've been improving my wardrobe on it! [Laughter]

KEVIN: And going to swankier restaurants!

DB: I see some pieces like the picture of Dodie and Dennis—that's in the elevator of Wheeler Hall in UC Berkeley—from the New Narrative Conference. The pieces all seem to be so evocative.

KEVIN: It's like an amazing way to look back at your life.

DODIE: This is all through him, that there are *any* portraits of me at all!

KEVIN: She doesn't like having her picture taken. That's like my favorite thing to do! [Laughter] And my own practice of it happened when Kathy died. I hadn't used a camera very regularly in the '90s because it just seemed so pointless. But I said, "I don't have a single picture of Kathy at all!" And that brought me to taking photographs, click, click, click. Memorializing, I guess, in a different way.

So besides writing about art, the two of us have turned to art practices ourselves. If ever I wind up having nothing more to say, which I don't really, I can just take more photographs of you, Daniel, and they'll go into the museum!

DB: And other boys who will agree to take off their clothes for you.

KEVIN: Yes! Because I'm Kevin Killian, and it's all good fun! But do you know Dodie sold a piece to the Vancouver Museum? Can you imagine? She never made a work of art in her life! Except that she was, of course, the premier graphic artist of New Narrative.

DODIE: I was a horrible graphic artist! But yeah, I was. I had access to the modes of production! [Laughter]

DB: Are you doing more visual work now?

DODIE: No, I don't have any other ideas! I'm writing a blog post for Artforum that should be up in a couple of days, if I can send it to them tomorrow. It's about photographs I took in Kevin's hospital room. So that's kind of art, by phone photographs. It's kind of a weird article, but he seems to think that I'm making it work.

KEVIN: The show in Bellingham had Dodie's big picture in it. But for me it isn't any of my photographs, but the poem drawings that I've been making ever since [artist] Ugo [Rondinone] told me to. They're selling them for $1,250, baby!

DODIE: But they specialize in the San Francisco and Vancouver poetry scene and art scene. So it makes sense, right?

KEVIN: We won't have many buyers.

DB: You just need the right buyer.

DODIE: Yes, we all just need the right one. ✄

....

Daniel Benjamin is the co-editor of The Bigness of Things: New Narrative and Visual Culture *(Wolfman Books) and lives in Oakland.*

THE HAND

INGRID ROJAS CONTRERAS

He had asked her to stay, to remain. He held her hand for an hour. The two palms sweated together, and for so many years. Their fingers fused. They daydreamed about the silver line of the blade, how the severed wrist would spew its blood, just like a person who'd taken a drink and was then surprised by a joke. One of them—him, they decided—would have to go on about their business holding the other person's hand. In time, her hand that wasn't his would rot and fall in a wet flop. They were unsure, however, if the organism they called "her hand" was hers. It felt like his body was the one breathing life into the fused hands, but then the feeling reversed. Under these conditions, severing the hand represented a risk. Who knew which body, hers or his, having been disconnected, would one day try to reach for a door and fall instead into a pile of hair and bone and then rise in a cloud of skin dust.

THE UNFINISHED QUESTION

INGRID ROJAS CONTRERAS

To capitalize on the wreck, the two surviving members of the office numbered, catalogued, and organized the loss. There was a spreadsheet of bonuses and negatives. Red numbers flashed across the screen. They climbed the mountain of ash. There were desk drawers breaking the surface of the ash mountain at the top. Inside were: a set of keys to the printer room. A tin of mints. The whole building had fallen. The printer room and the printer were both gone, buried with the rest of the unrecovered bodies, the collapsed brick, drywall, and wooden beams. Were the keys a positive or a negative? If you located the keys to a lost place had you located anything at all? The two members argued with hands at their hips at the crest of mountain that was the wreck, that was the burial. Should the keys be coded green or red? A breeze came just as they felt they would make up their minds. The air felt cool and refreshing. Even the smell of fire, even the distant wailing, felt like something that could happily carry them over into the unfinished question. ✄

....

Ingrid Rojas Contreras is the author of the novel Fruit of the Drunken Tree *(Anchor), and is Visiting Writer at St. Mary's College.*

ISLAND OF BEGINNINGS

LYDIA CONKLIN

On Wednesday night, after operating on the six-foot sunfish, Posey visited Island of Beginnings. The bar was across the street from the aquatic laboratory where Posey now worked. At eleven she left the office, crossed the Alewife Brook Parkway, jumped the guardrail, and slipped down the bank of wet, dead leaves. The bar made a triangle with her Soviet bloc apartment building and her fluorescent-lit workplace. Life in Fresh Pond was a joke with its battered malls and rotaries on the way to the city, which was really just Cambridge and not much of a city at all. But, somehow, this was real life. She'd separated from her husband, Ben, left him in San Francisco with its bright fruit and misty marijuana smoke and moved to a cement brick of a building with cruise ship windows and ceilings that grazed her scalp. She'd accepted a temporary position at the lab, where the manager had known her mother, because she couldn't find a job as a veterinarian. She missed working with cheery dogs and cats. Her job now was more stressful, but more important, too. She had to remember that she was contributing to a lasting environmental impact.

Posey had grown up just a mile away. She'd seen the sign for the bar as a child, passing through Fresh Pond with her mom, who had died a few years ago from a heart attack, the organ residually weak from a pre-Posey cocaine addiction. The fact that her mother had been around so recently left Posey with the feeling of lingering at summer camp after all her friends had been collected.

The bar's logo had stuck in her mind for three decades: the blocky angles of the Easter Island face, the Roman-style capital letters, the missing N in *beginnings*. She'd imagined it as a secret fortress for adults, and had planned to visit as soon as she was able. Now that she was divorced and nearly forty and living again in Cambridge, she guessed she qualified.

As a kid, Posey had imagined a life-sized Easter Island man installed in the bar, his stone-colored profile the texture of springy flesh. You could ask him the future and he'd reply honestly. You could lean against his cheek, pressing into his spongy granite, siphoning comfort.

Island of Beginnings was a freestanding concrete chunk with neon signs glowering in its murky interior. The soupy shape of Posey's reflection bobbed on the window as she approached. She couldn't wait to get a drink; to charm whatever guy was in there—she wouldn't be picky. She hoped to give the illusion of beauty, though she felt like shit. That morning she'd bungled the weekly procedure to remove encroaching settlements of tumors from the sunfish, an aggressive strain of contagious cancer that was exterminating bony fish all over the southern Atlantic. Posey had been charged with keeping this sunfish alive long enough so the scientists in the lab could solve his illness. They were modifying the genes of the jellyfish that passed on the cancer-causing fungus, so they could release a raft of fungi-resistant jellies back into the oceans to breed out the carrier population. Then sunfish and oarfish and swordfish across the ocean could dine safely once again. Or anyway, that was the idea.

Posey had never worked for the larger good of the environment before, and she savored the idea that she might help an entire species, an entire ecosystem, the entire ocean, just with diligent, mindless surgeries.

166   She relished that her simple, repetitive work would prevent bladders of jellyfish from cluttering the waves, crowding out delicate tropical fish and sea turtles and otters with their unchecked proliferation. But the sunfish's growths were hairier to remove than the standard-issue fatty tumors she'd pulled from golden retrievers for years. She'd have to repeat the operation tomorrow. To top it off, the lab manager had reported that the grant money was drying up. This wasn't shocking, as the public was cooling on genetic modification, even when it might prevent an apex predator from dying off and an ecosystem from collapsing. In a way, this was some relief, because the guinea pig fish was not happy. Weekly lumpectomies did not make for a healthy lifestyle. But even though Posey had known her job was temporary, she didn't know what she'd do without it.

She needed to have fun, meet people, maybe even have sex. Sex was good, right? Sex lightened moods. She'd spent every night working long hours in the lab and soaking in gray bathwater in her dreary apartment after, reviewing fish disease in textbooks with water-stained pages because she hadn't worked on marine life since graduate school. She needed to get out, even if just to across the street. This could be her first step socially: an easy, low-key bar. She'd accept a free drink and charm a grateful man. Next week maybe she'd take the train to Boston and meet someone more like Ben.

Island of Beginnings featured poured concrete floors with a bar along one side. Patsy Cline drooled from a jukebox in the corner. Two men slouched on their stools watching a bartender cut limes with unnecessary precision. Posey expected the men to say hi or at least smile. A woman's presence should cheer a place like this: the rare possibility of getting laid. One man glanced up. The other peered aggressively into a cup of dairy.

Sometimes Posey forgot that she'd emerged on this side of her marriage middle-aged. That she'd grown a potbelly and her hair was stringy from years of dying it what she had thought until recently was a striking crimson. Her skin, which had once been soft in a good way, in a childishly silky way, was now pricked with yawning pores and soft in a rotten way. Like an apricot that's technically safe to eat but inspires no appetite in any living person.

The bar was grimmer than she'd expected—clean but barren, like a soundstage for a moody man to contemplate his failed life. Posey wanted to retreat to her miniature apartment, hide up to her neck in steaming bathwater. But now that everyone had seen her walk in, she had to get one drink. The secret knowledge of her good work would shield her from any humiliation.

She slumped next to the man with the milky beverage. The cracked cushion of the stool puffed flat beneath her.

"I'll have what he's having."

The bartender began mixing with a sharp twist of his elbow. Affirming someone's drink choice was a way of making friends. She remembered that from her single days of yore. There weren't very many inroads when someone wouldn't look at you, but she liked the sense of returning to her innocent days, when any conversation could have led to a different marriage, a different life.

She'd chosen the man because he looked familiar. His weight was clustered around his hips and buttocks, which she remembered from her year of human medical training was supposed to be a healthy place to collect fat. A mole on his check was prominent and soft like a nipple, but his eyes were a warm, orange brown and somehow, though he was older than Posey, he had the face of a teen, beautiful and hard to impress.

"He's a little abrupt, isn't he?" Posey shrugged toward the bartender. This guy wasn't so kind himself. But she'd found through life that if you pointed out someone else's rudeness, another rude person would melt down.

"I guess." The man flicked his bangs from his eyes.

"Hey, do I know you?" He must've gone to school with her—his face made her feel like a kid again. A pretty kid.

"No," he said.

She was certain she must. "I'm Posey." Her voice came out sharper than she'd wanted, piercing the gelled air of the bar. The man looked startled. Posey's husband had only continued to find her amusing through their ten-year marriage because he'd known her since she'd been cute. New people found her alarming, took her sarcasm at face value. Maybe that's why she hadn't gone out since the divorce.

"Ben," the man said, squeezing the tips of her fingers. She stared, trying to decide whether he was messing with her. But how could he know? It wasn't like Ben was some super rare name, but still.

"Nice to meet you," she said, unable to repeat his name. The letters were too sharp on her tongue. She hadn't seen her Ben for months, had spoken to him on the phone only long enough to postpone paperwork out of a mutual fear of bureaucracy. She felt wrong saying his name to another man on another coast.

The bartender arrived with her drink. She took a long sip, then fought against spitting it back into the tumbler. "This tastes like Sprite and milk."

"It is," said New Ben, lifting his glass. "Brandy puff."

She could barely taste the brandy and the milk had a chemical edge. She suspected it had squirted from a hose hooked to the rim of the bar.

"Tasty," she said, and New Ben nodded without surprise. She sucked the mixture down as best she could.

Now that the thrill of entering Island of Beginnings had worn off and she was actually sitting here, Posey realized how depressing the situation was. In her apartment with her shipped books and worn-out rugs, she could pretend she was somewhere else. Back in college, maybe, when it was okay that the baseboards accrued dirt and hair. She could pretend her relationship with her Ben lay in the future. But here, with strangers, she had to recognize that it was over. That her skinny, hipster engineer husband was on the better coast, developing apps and sipping craft cocktails in exciting bars.

"So," New Ben finally said. "Your name is Posey."

The man next to New Ben leaned over. He was mostly bald, but had received what looked like pubic hair transplants at intervals along the crown of his head. A purple doughnut hugged the base of each follicle. He grinned and winked. "Sorry to interrupt, but I have to say it." He paused for effect. "That sounds like pussy."

"Well," Posey said. "It may come from the same Latin root."

Neither New Ben nor the pubic-headed man laughed.

"What brings you out here?" asked New Ben, perhaps inspired by his neighbor's interest.

She considered telling him she was desperate for human interaction, that she needed to replace the memory of her own Ben, her Irish wolfhound, and her beautiful, rent-controlled apartment in the Mission. But that would be rude. "The sign looked mysterious."

The pubic-haired man leaned back in his chair. "I can't believe it, Ben." He aimed a wobbly finger at her. "No offense, lady. But you actually want to do him."

Posey's mouth slotted open. She couldn't deny that she'd considered taking New Ben home. He reminded her of unpredictable kids from her high school, kids you wanted to hang around just to see what they'd do next.

"Shut up," New Ben said to the pubic-haired man, in a loud, clear voice. Posey hadn't realized how quiet he'd been until he spoke those words. Now his voice sang out sharp and accurate, each letter pronounced to its fullest possibility. The "s" finding its curl, the *up* pointing like a

170   finger. The pubic-haired man shrank back.

"I'm sorry," New Ben told her. "What did you say about the sign?"

Posey shook her head. "Really, I just work across the street."

"At Crispy's or the aquatic lab?"

"The aquatic lab."

New Ben leaned in. "You *do*?"

"You better believe it." She sounded so cheesy that she could've slapped herself.

"Smells like pussy over there," murmured the pubic-haired man, as if lost in thought. He seemed to have ceded the testosterone prize, content to make asides in the shadows.

"I think I've seen you go in there," said New Ben. "All professional, herringbone coat?"

Posey didn't own a herringbone coat. She couldn't even picture what herringbone was. But she nodded. This fake fashionable her could add to her intrigue.

New Ben fingered the nipple on his cheek. "I can't get enough of hearing about that place. There used to be this guy who worked there. Came in every day after work. Real funny guy. Ronnie or Donny or something. Then he died. Some story, right? From the chemicals, I guess. Or he might have moved. I forget."

Posey didn't think anyone had died at the lab. Mostly, she supposed, people feared the place because they were freaked out by the genetic modification of even an organism as basic and useless to humanity as a jellyfish. Posey didn't handle chemicals or modify genes. Her sole duty was to heal the sunfish. They wouldn't keep her on once funding was cut.

"It's not that exciting." Posey told herself she didn't care what people thought of her job. She was helping someone even if that someone was a fish. This man couldn't know that she was actually helping many more fish than that, perhaps the entire ocean. Her job was rare, because there were only two other ocean sunfish in captivity in America. That was part of why it was crucial that this one survived. Sunfish were the biggest species of bony fish, liver-colored jigsaws of body parts that suckled down thousands of nutrient-poor jellyfish to keep their weight steady at one ton. The sunfish looked like a chunk of a much larger fish, his head and body ill-proportioned to his tiny, feathered tail. The sunfish had the most pointless existence of any creature she'd encountered. For all the time they spent hunting jellyfish, their size was worthless. They barely had natural predators to bulk up against. Posey couldn't imagine an orca gnawing through the leather of its side, a shark choking down the crusty rind of its face.

Posey talked to the sunfish to keep her fingers steady while operating. She related her life with Ben: the way they'd molded pasta dough into new shapes—fingers! pumpkins! scrotums!—the way they'd walked the wolfhound until it lay in protest on a median strip, the secret crushes they shared, claiming sexy strangers as their property. Her patient, knocked out, seemed to listen. When she sewed him up, her old life stayed trapped in that humid pocket of fish flesh.

The creepiest thing about the animal, truly, was its eyes. They were rubbery and loose in the sockets. Sometimes when she'd finished removing a new front of pebbled tumors, had let the drugs wear off, and released the sunfish from the cords that held him afloat during procedures, she lingered against the tank, which had to be circular so jellyfish wouldn't snag in the corners. Her nose breath would fog the glass. She'd tell herself, Just one more revolution, then I'll go. And she'd watch the eye on her side pass again. And then she'd say, Just once more. The knobby pancake would pass again and she'd tell herself, Once more. Then, Once more.

"So," the pubic-headed man said, leaning close to Posey and New Ben. "What are you love birds up to tonight? Getting fresh over at the lab?"

New Ben palmed the back of the pubic-haired man's head, holding the skull in place as though he'd kiss it, and drove it into the rim of the bar. The man's eyes snapped shut as his temple met the bar; his mouth bursting open like an orifice you weren't supposed to see, his tongue tumbling out, so dry it didn't look alive.

The bartender's hand dangled at his hip, a snifter dripping on the floor. Blood bloomed on the bar without a sound. The man's skull clung to the lip of linoleum by the wound beside his ear.

"Ben, Jesus," the bartender said, his skin turning ashy as his expression stayed plain. "Now I have to call the cops."

The pubic-haired man popped his temple from the mess at the bar's edge and rolled to aim his face at the fluorescent tubes on the ceiling. His head moved as though it were disembodied from his stiff, diagonal body, a lonely skull flopping in the spilled brandy and blood.

"Don't be a prick, Clarence."

But the bartender dialed anyway. New Ben got up. On his way to the door he turned to Posey. "Nice to meet you." His face was unlined and innocent, the face a teenager showed his mother.

Then Posey was alone with the bartender and the bleeding man. She didn't want to wait for the police. She didn't want to be ignored by the bartender or harassed by the pubic-haired man with his dented skull. She didn't want to go home, either. The idea of floating in her bathwater now, knowing so much was happening a few yards from her window, would have been so lonely.

Across from the jukebox was a corner with a family of spare stools. That was where the Easter Island man would be if he were real, his glutinous shoulders melting into the floorboards. Posey pictured his stony jowl quivering, his lips ordering her to follow New Ben.

She was giving herself permission through her childhood fantasy, which was pathetic. But in this new life in a strip mall wasteland, floating every night in a soup of dead skin and fake red hair, a figment's advice was the best she could hope for. New Ben had put himself at risk for her. Even if the risk was misguided and immoral, no man had paid so much attention to her since her husband, and she couldn't walk away from the feeling.

✳   ✳   ✳

Outside the bar, New Ben scrambled up the slope. At each step he slid back, surfing the dead leaves, padded hips swiveling. He turned to Posey with sleepy eyes. "Care to join my great escape?"

They scaled the embankment. Island of Beginnings had not been built for foot traffic. The parking lot was around back and led directly onto Route Two, so you could transition from drinking to freeway driving in under ten seconds.

When they crested the slope, Posey realized they didn't have anywhere to go. She was used to the city, where if you got kicked out of one bar because your voice was too loud or your uncoordinated husband knocked over a potted fern, you could scale the next hill to another bar, then another, then a nightclub. You could stop by this friend's house in the Haight, that friend's house in the Richmond. You could buy juju fish at a convenience store. You could get to the bakery by four, scarf a sourdough boule full of cranberries and walnuts, fresh and gooey in its bubble of crust.

That was the joy of life when you were in love and thought it would last forever, with no talk of children and routine dipping into a drag. Then Ben met the young software engineer, and that was the end. Now the two of them were in Posey's apartment with Posey's Irish wolfhound and Posey's ratty rugs. Maybe it was chilly in the Bay, and Ben had made a fire in the woodstove they'd never tested. And here Posey was in a maze of crossed highways and gas stations and low-income housing on

174 the greasy border between Arlington and Cambridge and this was just how it was. She'd make the best of it. She'd squeeze something from the night. New Ben wasn't bad looking. He was a quintessential man.

"So," Posey said, on the edge of the highway. "What was that about?"

"What was what about?" New Ben leaned on the guardrail and lit a cigarette.

"Were you defending me? From Mr. Fancy Hair?" It was risky to push at the limits of someone's affection for you so early, but that was how Posey had gained friends in the past. Maybe the tactic still worked.

A square of white lit New Ben's eye, and he looked even more like a little boy. His cheeks flushed, turning even his nipple mole ruddy. "What do you think?"

Posey wanted to lean against his soft coat. Alewife Brook Parkway was practically dead, just one station wagon limping by in the furthest lane. Together, they watched the highway like a sunset. "Shouldn't we get out of here? Won't you get in trouble?"

"Gary won't press charges. He was asking for it."

"Are you sure?" Gary hadn't appeared too concerned for his health, but he couldn't be entirely unfazed about having his head split open.

"We have a what's it called. A dynamic." He shielded his cigarette as a motorcycle rushed by. "So what do you do over there?"

"I promise I won't infect you." Posey wiggled her fingers at him. He peered at them impassively, making her feel like an alien. Then he laughed, slowly, like he was trying to figure her out.

"Funny lady."

She felt her cheeks go red, which was amazing. She hadn't experienced embarrassment in ages. With Original Ben she'd been so beyond that. She'd known he had a crush on the new engineer a year before their marriage ended. He hadn't concealed his feelings, as though Posey were his buddy instead of his wife. When he'd finally asked her to move out she'd been too relieved to feel anything.

"Sorry for all the questions," Ben said. "I have a fascination with the place. It's like the only thing in Fresh Pond."

"Your friend Gary seemed to suggest we head over there." Posey heated at the reference to Gary's remark. She was putting sex on the table, if obliquely.

"I'd love to." He said it like a kid mentioning he enjoyed ice cream, wide-eyed and hopeful as a truck tinkled past. "I hear there's all kinds of crazy stuff in there."

"Oh yeah," Posey said, though there wasn't much. The animals, maybe, were of interest. There were otters and leopard eels, and a manatee with a bumpy, brain-shaped head named Mixed Nuts. The genetic modification was the most science-fictiony work they did, but it was invisible. They didn't have eels with two heads or an otter with the face of a human baby.

"You don't want to just come over my place?" Posey toed an oily puddle bordering the parkway.

Before Ben spoke, his eyes shifted, navigating this turn. "Maybe after?"

Posey led Ben across the freeway and up to the concrete pad around the lab. She unlocked the door with her keycard. Inside, a janitor swirled a mop in a sunny yellow bucket, but she knew from her late nights that he worked top down. He'd be gone any minute.

"I never thought I'd come in here," Ben said. "With a girl, no less."

Posey snorted. "Hardly a girl." But she was flattered.

As they crossed the mauve carpet to the back of the building, Posey saw the lab through Ben's eyes. The halls could've belonged to a regular office building, though behind each door was an animal stuck in the green gel of seawater, awaiting examination.

Smells like pussy. Posey had discredited Gary's assessment. After

176 all, he was drunk. He was no scientist. And he had pubic hair on his head. But he was right. The smell in these hallways was undeniably of sex. The connection made her shiver in her underwear.

"Not too shabby," Ben said, tapping a factory painting of a seal with eye makeup, flapping a seductive flipper.

Finally they reached her research room. She fumbled for the keys. She hardly knew this guy, and the janitor had left. She'd show him the sunfish quickly, and then she'd bring him to her apartment, where there were more people around. They'd be cozier there, anyway.

When she leaned down to unlock the door, Ben bumped into her. She felt the full length of his body against her.

He seemed spacey enough that it could have been an accident, but the possibility existed that he was letting her know that he wanted her. His body had felt good. She hadn't felt that kind of intense warmth in months, maybe even a year. When Original Ben had first met the engineer, there had been a flurry of activity. He'd come home hard every day, pounced on her even when she wasn't in the mood, but even those times she'd warmed up. One day, it stopped. After a few frigid months, he requested the separation.

In her office, the sunfish floated horizontally near the base of the tank. She was surprised to feel concern bubble up. But it was one o'clock in the morning. The sunfish had to rest sometime. He was sick, after all, standing in for all his siblings and cousins that were even sicker out there in the dark sea.

"God that thing's hideous." Ben approached the tank as the sunfish rose.

The fish was flat and warty. He barely seemed three dimensional, yet he was also fat. He slurped poisonous sea nettles and men o' war as though they were delicious sips of pudding. And he was infiltrated with a cancer worse than the one that had nearly decimated the Tasmanian devil. But he didn't look hideous right now. He was magnificent, scales **177** gleaming, eyes so alert they were nearly intelligent.

Ben leaned his face in close. Then he clattered a fist against the glass.

"Hey," Posey said.

Ben pounded the glass again. She swore there was a vibration in the water.

"Cut it out." Anger frothed in her chest, thicker than she would have thought possible. She wanted to jump him.

"I'm just saying hi."

"He's sick." Posey's voice was a desperate whine.

"I want to see the show." He banged again, this time harder.

Posey grabbed his wrists and wrenched him from the tank. They stared at each other. His nipple mole twitched. He smelled musky, and his wrists were live and sinewy in her grip. These were the fists that had slammed Gary and abused the sunfish's tank. They were wild, unpredictable hands, hands that excited Posey. He leaned toward her, his breath heating her cheeks.

"Show me what you do in here."

"I operate." Her power over the ocean surged through her.

"Show me." The minute Ben slipped from Posey's hands she wanted to catch him again. She wanted to push him on the floor and do the things to him that Gary had predicted. He waited, hands on hips.

She could perform tomorrow's operation now, but that would take at least two hours, and then it would be three in the morning. They wouldn't get back to her apartment until almost dawn, and she had to be at work at nine.

Ben's eyes were bright and interested. The sunfish was groggy from the surgery earlier. She could sedate him and cut him. She wouldn't have to go through with the full surgery. After all, she opened him every week. This was an easy way to impress Ben, and then they'd have plenty of time at her apartment.

They stepped onto chairs at the edge of the tank. Posey lowered the cords from pulleys above the rim. The sunfish was even easier to catch than usual, his senses dull with fatigue. She cranked the lever and drew him to the surface. He lay there, silvery water sliding off his scales.

Posey injected him with the sedative, then pulled on her gloves and disinfected his flank. She lifted a scalpel from her tray of tools and pushed through the stony flesh. She lined the incision up with the thin white scars from where she'd cut before, some of the marks still puckered and red. She separated the flaps of skin with clips. She used the scalpel as a pointer to indicate the beaded tumors.

"Wow," said Ben, hovering close. "I never knew what cancer looked like."

The first time Posey had seen cancer was inside a Labrador. That wasn't even the point of the surgery, which had been the extraction of a swallowed pencil, but the tumors had fascinated her. Rubber golf balls mushrooming for no reason beside working organs. She never got them out of her mind. Sometimes, at the end of her life with Original Ben, she'd wished she could snip that young engineer as cleanly from the body of their marriage, incising the tissue around her slender shoulders and transferring her to a bin of surgical waste.

Ben looked on with awe, and she was proud. Original Ben had never been interested in her stories from the clinic. She'd shared every gem: the dog that kicked her during neutering, trying to save his balls. The ferret that grew a calcium horn. The guinea pig that could squeak the words *I love you*. Original Ben had never even laughed or agreed a story was weird. But this Ben peered into the fish with fascination.

"This fish is the center of my world." She didn't want the operations to stop. She wanted the jellyfish tweaked and released, the sunfish saved—this one, and all of them. Her chest filled with the steam of pride.

Ben's eyebrows wrinkled, that sneering teenage look that so appealed to her. She set her gloved hand on his shoulder and leaned toward him even as he inched away. That's when she realized, so close up, that she *did* know him. He'd gone to high school with her—that was right. He'd been tiny for his age, and he hadn't had the nipple then. He'd prowled the fringes with headphones clamped over his hair while she laughed with her beautiful friends. She was the funny one in her group, plain in the face, but beauty had lapped onto her from the shiny hair of Lisa and Jenny and Megan. Ben must've watched her. The memory swelled her confidence, and she met his lips, which were wet and full; let feeling bloat in her. Tonight she'd break the seal, would start to live again. Her finger strayed to the nipple on his cheek, which was as velvety as she'd hoped. She let out a sound. She'd aimed for a sexy purr, but instead she released a deeply pleasured honk, the final cry of an erotic session, not the first.

Ben pulled away with a startled look. She understood from his face that he wasn't coming home with her. He couldn't handle seeing her with her hand up to her wrist in a fish, gabbing about how much she loved breaking open an animal again and again. And he didn't recognize her. She was too remote from that chatting, silly girl.

"Sorry." Ben glanced at the sunfish, as if apologizing to the unconscious creature, and stepped off the chair. "I'm sorry. I have to go." He backed out of the room, his face ruined with concern.

Posey was left on the chair alone. She tried not to cry. Other people's concern for her always made her cry more than her own misfortune. The first time she'd cried about her divorce was when she told a friend.

But she didn't know Ben, so why should she care if he pitied her? She considered Gary, smashed on the bar. Why had she followed a man who'd committed an act of spontaneous violence in front of her? She remembered growing up in the wake of her mother's drug addiction, how once, walking in Boston, a man had grabbed her mother and called her a slut. He'd waved a box cutter around by its orange handle. Posey worried they'd be killed, but he swung the blade back and sliced his own eyebrow in half. "Do you regret it now?" he asked. Her mother's face had gone gray as a towel. Posey should have known better. She'd learned early what lay under the surface in some men.

She turned back to the sunfish, to the bright growths inside him. She couldn't believe she'd cut him for Ben. She'd put him at risk and so, too, the future of the ocean. She had to finish the surgery tonight; make up for what she'd done. She was wide-awake anyway.

Before she began the removal, she peered into the open fish. She wanted to hug him, but he was two thousand pounds. So she leaned awkwardly over him, enjoying the surprising spring of his flesh.

The sunfish needed her. Though he would die even if she kept pace on the surgeries, for now she was holding him back from the edge. She would do this job for as long as she could. Then, when it was time, she'd go. She didn't have to stay in Fresh Pond if she didn't want. This life could be an interlude. She could even return to San Francisco.

She leaned closer so she was only a few inches from the sunfish's eye, turning back and forth in fear. ✄

Lydia Conklin is a Stegner Fellow at Stanford University. Her fiction has been published in Tin House, The Southern Review, The Gettysburg Review *and other publications.*

LAWRENCE FERLINGHETTI:
THE LATIN AMERICA NOTEBOOKS

MAURO APRILE ZANETTI

"He traveled a lot and he traveled light. He always carried a raggedy Pan Am bag about the size of a large toaster, in which he packed a change of underwear and an old navy tie in the unwanted event that a tie might be required somewhere, and he didn't want to embarrass his host. And he always carried small notebooks, which he filled with images, poems, political observations, character sketches."

These are Nancy J. Peters's words portraying her business partner and lifelong friend, Lawrence Ferlinghetti. Her tribute to San Francisco's first Poet Laureate was paid on the occasion of Ferlinghetti's 100ᵗʰ birthday, and celebrated the official proclamation from the city of San Francisco (March 24: Ferlinghetti Day) in a packed City Lights Bookstore, with crowds of every generation lining up outside on Columbus Avenue, and all over North Beach.

Peters depicts Ferlinghetti as a tireless globetrotter who "just happened to be present at so many watershed events of his century while they were happening." The Ferlinghetti Century, indeed! The list of historic events he witnessed is pretty long, but just to mention a couple: the Normandy invasion, and Nagasaki a few weeks after the bomb leveled the city. (A recent exhibition at the Harvey Milk Photo Center showcased some of the photographs Ferlinghetti took as a young navy officer in

182 Cherbourg.) Peters continued listing milestones of Ferlinghetti-being-present: "In the wake of the Cuban revolution he was in Havana. During Nicaragua's struggle for autonomy he was in Managua. During the May '68 insurgency in France, he was in the streets of Paris while students were scrawling radical poetry on the walls." And his travels continued for years, all across the United States, Europe, Russia, North Africa, and Australia. Peters reminds us that some of the greatest souvenirs "the People's Poet" brought back to San Francisco from around the world were "dissident poets like Yevtushenko and Voznesensky to perform for huge audiences, and good poetry to translate and publish. His choices and his art opened public space for new voices, censored voices, foreign voices."

And from every voyage, Ferlinghetti brought back notebooks, where new ideas unfolded with drafts of stories and, most of all, lots of drawings, masterfully sketched, often in journals made of artisanal vegetable fibers from Oaxaca, paper on which ink hypnotically flows and expands while brushstrokes playfully scrape shades into shapes. The best way to visualize, in Ferlinghetti's own words, "a reporter from Outer Space [covering] the strange doings of these 'humans' down here, sent by a Managing Editor with no tolerance for bullshit"—is to read his book *Writing Across the Landscapes 1960–2010 Travel Journals* (New Directions, 2015). Thanks to this publication, edited by Giada Diano and Matthew Gleason, we can understand Ferlinghetti's work "in the tradition of D. H. Lawrence's travels in Italy or Goethe's Italian journeys"; the well-known "clericus vagans" who tries to seize the day with the same urgency of a bullfighter: notes, ideas, puns, quotes, characters, faces, landscapes, masks, and animals interwoven from page to page. Going through these travel journals, we can witness, almost like walking in real time with him across more than five decades in his "walkabout in the world," how he was writing and sketching with his distinct lightness, style, curiosity, and excellent sense of humor. "I was just a dog walking the streets, observing and noting everything happening around him." That's the quintessential self-portrait of the young artist Ferlinghetti has described to me many times, but it is also the mark of his creative process.

Latin America, and specifically Mexico, has been a *ritornello* in Ferlinghetti's lifetime score, its rhythms provided by his many travels, plethora of acquaintances, and the most diverse kind of friends, a never-ending volcanic activity of insurgent art and outstanding poetry. From the first journal (1960) to the most recent (2010), the voice and the sign of Latin America plays the prologue and the epilogue.

Beyond so many words spread like seeds—spoken ones, written ones, read, reread, interpreted, sung and performed, again and again—the lyrical heart of Ferlinghetti's poetry actually lies in the bosom of his drawings and sketches. Here's the origin of the voice's timbre, and of the *little boy* eternal in every human being, particularly so in the poet. These notebooks are Ferlinghetti's artistic magma, what Antonin Artaud—who wrote *Mexico and Voyage to the Land of the Tarahumaras*—called *"la parole avant la parole"* (the word before the word). If, according to Heraclitus's aphorism, *the God whose Oracle is in Delphi neither indicates clearly nor conceals but gives a sign*, we can assume it's not just nature that loves to hide, but sometimes art as well.

Latin America for Lawrence is not just a geographic destination, but also an aesthetic category of contrast: dictatorships and revolutions; ancient rituals and masks, and modern, Western ones; joy and despair at their peak. The notebook excerpted here is dedicated to the Mayan gods—an homage to the pre-Columbian civilization and its mysterious signs. This physically small notebook is dated 2004, coinciding with an exhibition ("Courtly Art of the Ancient Maya") organized at the Fine Arts Museums of San Francisco, where Nobel Peace Prize Laureate Rigoberta Menchú gave a special presentation.

Ferlinghetti's sketches are charming because of their simple touch, incisive gestures, and unflagging humor. No matter if it is a figure or a mask, a statue or an animal, each is a monument contained in a few lines. It would be a dream to one day see a whole catalog dedicated to Lawrence Ferlinghetti's notebooks. No words, and no explanations, just the golden silence of the poet's joyful signs, following in the Sicilian saying, the best word is the one you never say. ✄

. . . .

Mauro Aprile Zanetti is a San Francisco author and personal assistant to Lawrence Ferlinghetti, with a background in independent filmmaking. The notebook excerpted in the following pages is reproduced at its original dimension of 4 ½ × 6 inches. For more information about Lawrence Ferlinghetti's art, visit ferlinghettiart.com.

MAYA

MAYA

Ferlinghetti '04

Aunque la mona se vista de seda, mona se queda.

Even if the monkey dresses in silk, a monkey she remains.

Mayans Monkey
with cocoa-
pods

Yo soy Libra.

"God Number 13"
The Patron
of Arts
+ Writing

" Blood Letting
Ritual
&
Lady Xok"
(with Rope of thorns
being drawn thru
her tongue.

Royal
Man
+
Wife~
chiapas

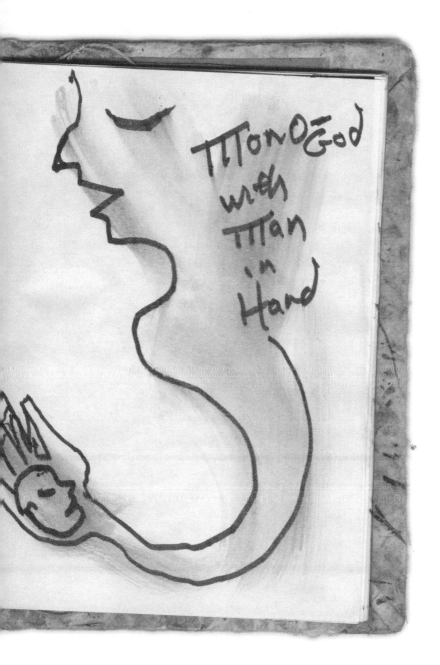

TITON OF GOD
with
TITAN
in
Hand

IN LOVE WITH A WOMAN

LADY NESTOR GOMEZ

I should die in miscommunication
breed fantasies unregulated, losses innumerable
Mejor hablar español
o componerme en nahuat

I could speak and not offend

I would stop a symphony
and find closure
erase bus stops
and listen to my sister, the violent rain

waiting for your seven days

This isn't a poem of love
or hate
but our days traveling in gray sand
black night beaches and post-birthdays

to speak to you

I could hide and not love
die in anonymity
vanish in the '80s with the rest of my ghosts
but I can't stop searching engines for your name

our last two hours in memory always remain

one, two, three feels like love
a tree broke that morning
nimeztneki
and fell onto the road

MAKING A DENTIST APPOINTMENT

LADY NESTOR GOMEZ

I chipped my tooth and I think depression did this

too little Sensodyne

not being wasteful, drinking all the soup

the enamel from the bowl kissing the enamel of my tooth

love not meant to be

one was left broken

the other was left blue

the damage permanent because these are my last teeth

the damage permanent because neglect is grounds for removal

Why is it that I will brush my teeth after every meal in a "shithole" country

but never give a fuck in a rich one?

Why does a single chipped tooth make me question my immortality?

Where have my friends gone?

And now I worry that my rich country dentist wants all my money

because I don't love my teeth

Lady Nestor Gomez is editor-at-large at Asymptote Journal *and a translator of Salvadoran literature, and lives in Concord, California.*

IS SOMEONE GOING TO SAY SOMETHING TO THE WOMAN CRYING ON BART?

ANDREW ROE

S he can't be seen, only heard, but she is somewhere on the other side of the crowded train. Dark outside, light inside, moving first through downtown San Francisco and next tunneling through the bay and all that water before then emerging above ground in West Oakland, all the cranes and trucks and ghostly industry. End-of-day faces, commuter faces. So much proximity and opportunity and yet. And the woman cries. And because she can't be seen, it is not clear if she's on the phone and has received recent news, or if the periodic weeping signals a remembrance, a recollection of some previously known woe. Sounds youngish. But who knows? Sobs short and long. Like bursts of music, never certain of its duration, only its intent. Somewhat faint but definitely audible. No one seems to notice. Or wants to notice. It is just another day, another anonymous evening ride, and everyone wants to get home.

Then—

The crying has stopped. Back to the metallic groans of the train and the track, the train and the track. No human sounds. Just now realizing the crying has stopped, but it could have been a while, perhaps several **201** minutes, thoughts have a way of running along and consuming and shutting out everything else. Keep listening. Pay attention. How can we do more of this, be better at this? The woman could have stopped crying or she could have gotten off the train at the last stop. No one approached her, no one said a word. At least there was no observable evidence—visual, aural—of consolation. But it's possible that the woman would have rebuked any such advance, any stranger offering solace. People don't want to talk or touch or anything on public transportation. There are barriers, force fields that exist without us asking for them. Pretty sure it was crying, but now, in retrospect, it could have been laughing. Sometimes it's hard to tell the difference. ✄

Andrew Roe is the author of the novel The Miracle Girl *(Algonquin Books), a finalist for the Los Angeles Times Art Seidenbaum Award for First Fiction, and lives in Pleasant Hill, California.*

TO THE BAY BRIDGE

MATTHEW ZAPRUDER

I hate decoration

except on ancient fortresses

like the Alhambra

where many years ago

I took my darkness

but could not leave it

the blue tiles

were too bright

I loved them so

dazed in the hope

okay not right now

but maybe soon

life will become

less in the same

boring way interesting

out the gate I drifted

into narrow streets

that kept curving

always downward

until I turned

one final time

onto a street

and stood before

a little church

guarded by

a demon perched

above the door
forever to scare
the few believers
left into taking
shelter in the cool
shadows of weekly
mystification
I stood there
waiting for a solemn
diurnal ritual to end
so I could go inside
and touch the walls
and understand
as always nothing
I know it's probably
wrong to love
old movie theaters
in midwestern towns
cluelessly resembling
an Arab palace
in the mind
of the vice president
of the Rotary club
only a few faded
walls and minarets
remain surrounding
lions inside the lobby
nobly asleep in a slow
benevolent local
commerce dream
that business
once was young

204

here in the west
they finally built
the new bridge
across the bay
it glows in white
unadorned solicitude
as if it will never
become obsolete
driving across it
the electric buses
blink go warriors
in pure silent fog
and everyone agrees

Matthew Zapruder is the author of several poetry collections, most recently Father's Day *(Copper Canyon Press), as well as the book* Why Poetry *(Ecco), and is an associate professor at St. Mary's College of California.*

NEIGHBORS TALKING

LYDIA KIESLING

1.

Around the time we moved into our current place in San Francisco, things began accumulating in the front yard of an unoccupied house down the block. The house was more like a cottage, set well back from the street, and there was a long narrow patch of grass in front of it, which began to fill up with household items—lamps, chairs, and even heavy items of furniture like loveseats and desks. Eventually, I realized that these were the belongings of one of the people in the neighborhood who does not have stable housing, and who I was accustomed to seeing with a shopping cart and a collection of large suitcases that he would move painstakingly up and down a given block over a period of hours and days.

By now I have seen so many hauling trucks in front of this house that I can't remember whether I really witnessed, or just heard about, the first eviction of the man's trove of things. I am told by a neighbor that haulers had to hacksaw through the elegant Rubik's Cube the man had created out of the neighborhood's cast-off items. They threw the pieces into the truck, and then erected a tall plywood fence to keep further items from coming in. But the house continued to sit empty, and new things began to accumulate in front of and eventually beyond the plywood wall.

One day, I saw the man walking in the general direction of the house with a motorized pink Barbie Jeep held above his head, and felt something I can only clumsily describe as triumph on his behalf.

2.

Our landlord, who has owned a house on this block for decades, has a deep dislike of having his business known. He collects our rent check in person, and cautions me against telling neighbors or handy-people anything about the house or what we pay to rent it; he says everyone on the block likes to know everyone else's business. He is himself a talkative man, but wary of the effects of talking. So about him I'll just say that he is a good landlord and a kind person.

I, on the other hand, love knowing people's business, especially as it pertains to this block. My husband and I have lived on this block since we moved back to San Francisco seven years ago, first on one side of the block, in two different houses owned by the same woman, and for a year now on the other side, in the property of our circumspect landlord. For three years now, I have worked from home, which means I'm outside a lot, which means it's possible for me to collect more items of business than I had previously been able. I walk to the coffee shop; I walk to the grocery store; during periods of weakness I stand and stare at my phone under a sheltering bottlebrush tree on the corner of the block. This tree sits in front of a corner building, zoned for business, which has been empty since we have lived in the neighborhood. It is becoming a childcare center, I'm told, but it has been difficult for the owner to acquire the necessary permits to set it up.

Before we had this landlord, we had another landlord for six years, an elderly woman who loomed in our imagination the way an eccentric wealthy aunt in Victorian England might have done. She had a stormy temperament, and we had several baffling phone calls with her before a neighbor tactfully told us that she wasn't good in the afternoons. She also had a soft heart. When our first daughter was born, she sent us a check for $200 and, thereafter, Christmas gifts for the baby. She had no children but spoke of "heirs," and she assured us she had put in a good word with them in the event of her demise.

She told us she was born in the first of her houses that we lived in, a one-bedroom cottage built after the 1906 earthquake. We paid $1,800 a month to rent it at a time when the average rent for a one-bedroom in San Francisco was $2,700. After three years and the birth of our first child, we moved into the place she owned next door, which had two bedrooms. For this place, we paid $2,300 when the average rent for a two-bedroom in San Francisco was $4,500. Our landlady told us her father had made her buy the house when she was twenty-three, when what she really wanted to buy was a Thunderbird.

The people who had vacated this larger place did so because they had gotten a city loan for middle-income people and had, incredible in 2014, found a house that they could buy with the loan. Right when they were moving into the new house, the roof fell in and they had to fix it up. Then the man's elderly mother had to move in with them. Then the man died suddenly, leaving the woman sharing their long-awaited home with her mother-in-law. After this happened, she came to visit the house we now occupied—the garden she had made beautiful over fourteen years of renting with her husband. She took sprigs of what she explained was St. John's wort to decorate the room where they would hold his memorial.

3.

We got the call that our landlady had died when I was pregnant with our second child. Because of her prognostications about her own death, she had let us sign a three-year lease on which we had one year remaining. Her heir was a cousin, an older-sounding woman who lived in the north, in the direction of where my mother is from, a fact I tried to

208 work into conversation in case it was compelling. After several months the heir told us she didn't have the energy to be a landlord, even though in this case the role seemed limited to cashing checks from people who were too nervous to call her. Another cousin, the deceased landlady's nephew, was a realtor, and he was going to come and sort everything out. She assured us he would be kind.

The realtor-cousin drove a nice car and assured us, again, that he would be kind. He also told us some stories about our landlady, which seemed in keeping with what we knew about her. She collected cats and dogs and even a skunk in her house outside of the city, which the cousin was selling along with the house we lived in and the smaller one next door. When she died, there was evidently a man living in her basement whom she had met and invited in while walking her dogs. We became as reverent of the landlady's memory as if she had been our actual relative. They sent us her death certificate in the mail. From that we learned she had been younger than she looked. She had had three husbands and emphysema.

We looked at the current rental listings and home prices and we asked the heir what it would take for us to buy the house. In the night, the realtor-cousin stuck through our gate an estoppel form upon which he had written they were trying to get a number "like 950," although they listed the house at $750,000. He scheduled open houses and I stood pregnant and sullen in a form-fitting dress in the kitchen while visitors walked past. People would ask why we were leaving and I would say, "Well, we have a year left on our lease." This embarrassed some people; a few others said, "So what do you think of the neighborhood?" After a lot of agonizing, we offered to buy the house for its asking price, which we could not afford to do. We wrote a letter that described our love for the deceased landlady, and the Mother Goose stuffed animal she sent at Christmas. The house had chunky stucco walls and wall-to-wall carpeting and termite damage and our letter went on, at length and truthfully, about how much we loved living there.

The living area of the house was on the second floor, with windows that had an expansive view of the block and the adjacent neighborhoods. One day I watched from these windows as our neighbors' spirited dog sprinted down the street, chased by one of her owners. I saw my husband riding home from work on his bike and yelled out the window for him to turn around and assist with the rescue. Before this stretch of time in San Francisco, I had never lived in a single place longer than five years, and yelling out the window about the dog made me feel like I was part of something.

This dog's owners bought their house around the time our landlady died. We had gone to the open house out of morbid curiosity and discovered it came with a small house in the backyard wherein lived a tenant who is theoretically protected from eviction for legal reasons. She was sitting watching TV while streams of people went back and forth among her things and opened doors to poke around.

We eventually got to be friends with the house's new owners. They were both from other countries and had met on a work-study visa, fallen in love, and gotten married. Now they were applying for a green card that has been subject to delays. They have not been able to visit their families for years because they are too worried they won't be able to get back into the United States, even though their home is here, and their jobs and spirited dog.

4.

When we were scheming to try to buy the house we rented, it wasn't the house so much, but the idea of being tied to a place, to a neighborhood—to this particular neighborhood, which to me is the platonic ideal of neighborhood, the houses close together, densely

210 covering a block but still embodying, more or less, the house shape that I have been conditioned to admire. These houses have small backyards, sometimes full of lemon trees and birds of paradise, sometimes paved in concrete. They are painted in bright colors or they have faux-stone facing or they are beige and in need of a scrub. They are Mediterranean and Edwardian and Marina Style and Art Deco and Earthquake Shacks and what would have been Contemporary in the 1970s. There is a mix of small apartment buildings and single-family homes divided into two or three units. There are bottlebrush and ice plants and jade plants and wood pigeons. There are skunks who are fed by a man on the block, although this may be slander against him by another neighbor. The sidewalks are wide and perfect for little children to meander. When it's early and quiet, you can hear BART in the distance. On the one hand, it does not seem like too much to ask to live in a neighborhood like this. On the other hand, it seems fantastically entitled. From some vantage points, you can see the ocean.

The neighborhood is also considered to be one of the most racially and ethnically diverse neighborhoods in San Francisco. It is a place where teachers and mail carriers and flight attendants own houses, and looks from above like an embodiment of the relative success of the American experiment: people speaking many different languages living next to each other, going to the same library, and patronizing, more or less, the same businesses. Our landlady was white; the longtime landlady in the identical house adjacent was black; the house beyond that was owned by an Asian American family. Proximity should never be confused with friendship, but in a lot of places, even this proximity is rare.

There are reasons the neighborhood looks the way it does. From the old place's window, you could see a development across the main thoroughfare, where the houses are lovely bungalows and set further apart, on streets that curve and wend rather than lying out in a grid as they do on our side of the street. This housing park was built with a covenant that stated "No person of African, Japanese, Chinese or any Mongolian descent shall be allowed to purchase, own or lease any real property." Covenants like this were supposed to have been illegal after 1948, but when a black family bought there in 1959, they had to break into their own home to take occupancy. Another adjacent housing development, with larger houses on a different pattern, had the same covenant. When the first black resident bought there in 1957, someone burned a cross on his lawn. He was an assistant district attorney at the time; three years later, he was the U.S. Attorney for the Northern District of California; thereafter, a federal judge. When Willie Mays and his family moved into the tony neighborhood up the hill, someone hurled a bottle bearing a racist epithet through their window.

Our neighborhood, which falls between those developments, was a black neighborhood relative to most neighborhoods in San Francisco—60 percent black by the 1970s, when only 13 percent of city residents were black. By the time we moved here, the demographic proportions had changed. Once on the bus I overheard a passenger chatting to the driver, who was an acquaintance. They were both black, and they were talking about how different things were now. "I don't know who's here, but it's not us," the passenger said, and gestured to the rest of the bus, where there were mostly Asian American and a couple of white passengers, me among them.

There are a few people with insecure housing I see regularly in the neighborhood. One man, who is black, now has a place to live in another neighborhood, but this neighborhood is where he is from and he visits three days a week. He knows everything about the buildings on the main street, what businesses used to be there, who has moved away or died going back forty years. I remember reading a profile in a local paper a few years back about another man from the neighborhood.

212 He had special needs, and when his family died, he was left to depend on friends and neighbors, and sometimes sleep in the doorways of the businesses on the street. The overall percentage of people without housing has increased 30 percent in the last two years. The overall percentage of black residents in the city as a whole is now 6 percent, but black people make up a third of people without housing.

I am in a Facebook group for mothers in San Francisco that has more than ten thousand members. Sometimes women post on the group questions like, "If you have left the city, why?" The answer is often some version of "Too many homeless. Too dirty. Not safe." For a while, hate-reading these posts preoccupied me to an extent that I came to feel was unhealthy. Some members post to the group from homeless shelters.

5.

Shortly after the last open house in our deceased landlady's home, her cousin-realtor told us someone had offered to pay $831,000 in cash for the house, with no inspection and five days to close. After the sale the heir called me to say that she was "sorry we hadn't been able to make it work." I was aware she was now our landlord reference, so I held the phone away from my ear and said I understood and thank you when the sound of talking came to an end. There was some satisfaction that our presence in the house had probably reduced the number of offers they received.

After the sale closed, the new owner brought his wife over, since she hadn't seen the house when he had offered to buy it. We had been thinking of him as our enemy, but it turned out he was nice. He was born in the city—neither my husband nor I could say the same—and he and his wife and three children had squeezed into a one-bedroom condo prior to this. He and his wife spoke another language together. When we showed them around the house, he told me "I can't believe it. I own a house in San Francisco" with such gladness I actually felt happy for him. I see him all the time now to pick up our straggling mail, and I like to have one more person I know in the neighborhood.

The owner of our daycare, who bought a house nearby for over a million dollars, told me there are people who give short-term, high-interest loans if we wanted to try to buy something else. Friends who bought a place around the same time she did, also for more than a million dollars, told us they had a friend who gave them a loan at 1 percent, which let them make an all-cash offer, win the house, and immediately refinance to pay it back. This was interesting information, but it did not solve the problem of the amounts involved. Two of our friends, who have what we consider to be good but not astronomical salaries, recently bought a one-bed, one-bath for over a million dollars. They are good enough friends that we got in their business and they told us that with 20 percent down, their mortgage was around $4,800 dollars per month.

With a few months left on our lease, friends who lived on the other side of the block in a rent-controlled apartment experienced a terrible tragedy. When I condoled with them, they told me that they were going to move. The first thing they said after that was, "And we're going to get you guys into our place." *This is San Francisco*, I thought to myself, and eventually said to them. *The worst moment in a person's life and they are thinking about the housing angle.*

And that's what happened: they got us into their place. Our rent went up, but not very much, thanks to another kind, elderly landlord.

6.

Soon after we moved into the new place, I went on a bus organized by tenant groups and the Democratic Socialists of America (DSA) to ask the state legislature to repeal the Costa Hawkins Act, which, among

214 other things, prohibits rent control for single-family homes. I had time on my hands with a new baby, and a selfish personal investment in this issue, having until recently been a tenant in a single-family home. If memory serves, one of the attendees (white) carried a copy of Mao's Little Red Book; I carried the baby and felt bourgeois. After the assembly members debated the merits of repealing Costa Hawkins, we, the public, lined up to provide comment: our names, whether we supported the repeal, and whatever slogan we could fit in that would make us sound legitimate.

The other side was represented by a lot of people who said a repeal would interfere with their livelihoods, some of whom were more sympathetic than others. One woman said in accented English that she had cleaned other people's toilets and saved her money and had the right to do what she wanted with her house, and it was hard not to agree. In fact, many of the people providing comment on the opposing side would not, at one point, have been allowed to buy property in the neighborhoods adjacent to mine; many would not have been able to enter the United States at all until the Chinese Exclusion Act was repealed and national immigration quotas removed.

Thinking about housing in terms of identity does not seem like a policy solution, but identity has defined housing for the duration of our history, so it is hard not to. (Lately people make very free with the shorthand "Chinese investors," a group that is scapegoated along with "tech people" for the surge in cash purchases. It's a shorthand that feels peculiar in a city with a Chinese American population that comprises more than a fifth of the city, one that established itself in the face of decades of racist immigration policies.) But then came another voice from the opposing side, a white man who said as his public comment, "Housing is not a human right," and it was very easy to be against him.

In any case, they did not repeal Costa Hawkins that day.

Subsequently, the DSA and tenants rights groups find themselves in peculiar alliance with some landlords and suburban residents against a proposed zoning change that would make it easier to build new housing close to transit. The former point out that it will hasten gentrification and displacement; the latter fear for their property values and suburban way of life. They are allied against this bill, but not on the question of what might replace it.

It is difficult for me, with no policy knowledge, and contending with the conflicting statements of these shifting and unlikely coalitions, to form an intelligent opinion about housing. All I have is anecdata that adds up to nothing: my small collection of other people's business, first- and second- and third-hand. What I know is that the housing situation is, in a word, fucked. What I suspect is I am not far enough removed from the race- and class-based ideologies that have brought us all to where we are now to think clearly about it. What I know is that wherever my husband and I go next, we are a vector—the kind with a permanently warped sense of what constitutes affordable, with easy access to credit, with a desire for two bathrooms in something house-shaped and close to other things.

7.

Recently, another landlord on our block died. His children ousted his longtime tenant and sold the place, a one-bed, one-bath, for $975,000. "Imagine the Possibilities!" read the listing. The home had last sold for $52,500 in 1998. Renovations immediately commenced, and one of the neighbors told me that the new owners were planning to live in it. But a few weeks ago, I saw a staging truck parked out front, and on the sidewalk the telltale lines of neo-mid-century furniture you see on Redfin. Nine months after the sale it is for sale again, with three new bedrooms and a 1.4 million dollar price tag. ("Seems low," a neighbor said.)

We got a flier in the mail advertising the realtor services of our deceased landlady's cousin. There was a photo of the three houses she had owned, two of which we had once lived in, and a description of his prowess in getting these properties sold. Maybe that's the moment we decided to go.

San Francisco gave me my man and my two babies. The City and County of San Francisco, specifically, via my man, gave me two pregnancies that cost me a total of $150 each. It gave him twelve weeks of paid leave. It gave us the smell of eucalyptus and what I now know is St. John's wort. It gave us a glimpse of what it might feel like to stay. But we can't make it give us what it doesn't have to give. And we are lucky: we are going on our own terms.

8.

Last week I ran into a neighbor and we rode the light rail together downtown. He and his wife are teachers in the San Francisco Unified School District and have owned their house for a while. I told him we were moving away and he said he thought we were doing the right thing. I also asked him what the deal was with the vacant house that was always having debris hauled away from its yard. He told me he met the owner on the street recently and talked to him. He lives in another city, far away, and has no plans to do anything with the house. "Why would he?" my neighbor said. "Right now it can sit there like it is and appreciate in value. Everything here just keeps going up, up, up."

Lydia Kiesling is the author of the novel The Golden State *(Picador) and her work has appeared in* The New York Times Magazine, Slate, The Guardian, *and other publications.*

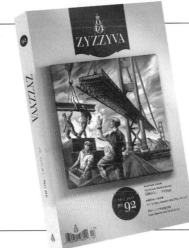

ORGANIC VODKA

MADE IN HUMBOLDT COUNTY, CA